D0275981

Mark Wigan

Thinking
Visually

adj. using thought or
rational judgement

adv. relating to seeing or
sight: visual perception

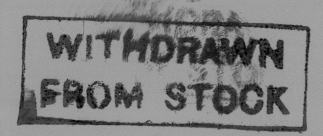

ava | **Academia**
the environment of learning

ava

AVA publishing SA
Switzerland

An AVA Book

Published by AVA Publishing SA

Rue des Fontenailles 16, Case postale, 1000 Lausanne 6, Switzerland

Tel: +41 786 005 109

Email: enquiries@avabooks.ch

Distributed by Thames & Hudson (ex-North America)

181a High Holborn, London WC1V 7QX, United Kingdom

Tel: +44 20 7845 5000 Fax: +44 20 7845 5055

Email: sales@thameshudson.co.uk

www.thamesandhudson.com

Distributed in the USA & Canada by:

Watson-Guptill Publications, 770 Broadway, New York, New York 10003

Fax: +1 646 654 5487

Email: info@watsonguptill.com

www.watsonguptill.com

English Language Support Office

AVA Publishing (UK) Ltd.

Tel: +44 1903 204 455

Email: enquiries@avabooks.co.uk

ISBN 2-940373-15-9 and 978-2-940373-15-4

10 9 8 7 6 5 4 3 2 1

Designed at the NEW Studio (TM)

Email: theStudio@NEW-online.co.uk

www.NEW-online.co.uk

Original text and photography by Mark Wigan

(with thanks to the students at Camberwell College of Arts)

Original book and series concept devised by Natalia Price-Cabrera

Production and separations by AVA Book Production Pte. Ltd., Singapore

Tel: +65 6334 8173 Fax: +65 6259 9830

Email: production@avabooks.com.sg

CONTENTS

Inspirations

Outsider Art

Experimental Workshop

Underground Urban Art

Printmaking

Collaboration

NEW STRATEGIES FOR THE ART OF ILLUSTRATION

'There is almost a revolution in illustration at the present time, and both old and young, teachers and scholars are in want of a handbook for reference when training to the new methods', wrote Henry Blackburn in *The Art of Illustration* in 1894 during the golden age of illustration. Over a hundred years later, *Basics Illustration: Thinking Visually* has been produced to provide a handbook for the new golden age of illustration. The *Basics Illustration* series seeks to encourage a new discourse within the discipline and act as a guide for professional illustrators and students alike.

There is a huge revival of interest in the art of illustration: from children's books, graphic novels, animation, books, toys, computer games to fashion, advertising, design, broadcast media and the internet. Illustrators are providing conceptual and narrative content in numerous media and contexts. Working independently, through agent representation or collaboratively in 'collectives', illustrators are now engaging with the global digital communications revolution, combining a wide range of both traditional and digital media and techniques. The new generation of illustrator operates globally, elucidating, informing, entertaining, interpreting, provoking, educating and intriguing.

'To speak of the education of an illustrator seems to me to give too much honour to an undesirable by-product of our age – specializations. To put first things first: the illustrator is an artist whose education knows no beginning and no end', commented Fritz Eichenberg in the *Illustrator's Notebook* in 1978.

Thinking Visually has been written with this open-ended approach in mind, reflecting the multidisciplinary nature of the subject and leading to new creative possibilities for illustration. Preconceptions, parameters and limitations of the profession of illustration are being constantly challenged as working processes, technologies and markets evolve. Many continue to create highly imaginative and exciting commissioned work. However, the new flexible generation of illustrators is creating self-driven projects incorporating entrepreneurial skills, taking responsibility and control of the whole process from concept to final product.

Thinking Visually acknowledges the expanded role of the illustrator as a flexible, transglobal, entrepreneurial producer of self-initiated projects. No matter what the context of work, the need for intelligent personal and original illustration remains paramount. The ability to think visually and the development of a personal visual language comes from learning the basics, being open-minded, hard work, sustained practice and taking risks. The first book in the *Basics Illustration* series, *Thinking Visually*, features the work of more than 100 international illustrators, educators and students. A wide variety of work demonstrating diverse visual languages, contexts, ideas, techniques and skills is featured. The handbook's aim is to introduce fundamental techniques, inspire, inform and act as a useful resource on international contemporary practice. *Thinking Visually* explores the importance of ideas, research, drawing and experimentation for the illustrator.

Contemporary illustrators from all over the world engaged in a diverse range of approaches to the discipline have contributed their artwork and commentaries on visual thinking, working processes and advice for students of illustration.

The handbook also features the work of recent graduates, present students and observations from educators past and present. The book is a window to leading-edge international practice and an educational tool featuring short exercises, methods, workshops, techniques, media, and historical and contemporary contexts.

Practical, contextual and intellectual issues fundamental to the discipline are all addressed. Creative thinking is explored via the experimental application of image-making with a broad range of media.

Spider diagram (below) by Mark Whitby
A diagram used to discover ideas and themes radiating from a project title.

Chapter one

EUREKA! – Analyses basic research strategies. Examples of spider diagrams, brainstorming and project maps, rough visuals, sketchbooks and scrapbooks are all used to illustrate the process of visualising ideas and building visual intelligence. International practitioners also reflect on their personal inspirations.

Chapter two

DRAWING – Examines the key skill of drawing, the synthesising of hand, eye and brain. Examples of drawings from life, the imagination and visual memory are presented. The influential area of 'Outsider Art' is explored. Portraiture, composition and the manipulation and construction of imagery are introduced.

Chapter three

PLAYTIME – Explores how the process of risk taking and experimentation can help extend the illustrator's personal visual vocabulary. In Experimental Workshop, illustrators explain their diverse working processes along with examples of some of their work.

Chapter four

POINTS OF VIEW – Introduces visual interpretations of text and the illustrator's intent within a wide range of contexts, including Caricature, The Decorative, Social Comment, Reportage, Underground Urban Street Art, Storytelling (comics, graphic novels, children's books and visual essays) and Fantastic Worlds.

Chapter five

TOOLS OF THE TRADE – Reveals the huge range of image-making tools utilised by today's illustrators, including printmaking, photography and digital media.

Chapter six

METHOD IN THE MADNESS – In Learning Through Making, international illustrators give their advice on what students of illustration need to learn. Examples of visual thinking project briefs are provided, collaborative working processes explored and there is a canon of key artists and illustrators.

This book introduces different aspects of illustration via dedicated chapters for each topic. Each chapter provides numerous examples of work by leading artists, annotated to explain the reasons behind the choices made.

Key illustration principles are isolated so that the reader can see how they are applied in practice.

Clear navigation

Each chapter has a clear strapline to allow readers to quickly locate areas of interest.

Introductions

Special section introductions outline basic concepts that will be discussed.

Quotes

Key points are elaborated on and placed in context through the use of quotes.

Examples

Projects from contemporary illustrators bring the principles under discussion alive.

34 / 35

Outsider Art

Idiosyncratic, magical and obsessive, Visionary, Folk and Outsider Art have proven to be a powerful influence on the development of art and illustration.

Historical precedents include the imaginative works of Arcimboldo, Bomarzo, Goya and Bosch. The visionary tradition of naïve and obsessive art continued with Henri Rousseau, Morris Hirschfield, Ferdinand Cheval, Simon Rodia, Madge Gill, Adolf Wölfli, Henry Darger and Howard Finster. In 1945, Jean Dubuffet invented the term 'Art Brut' to describe 'artistic works such as paintings, drawings, statues and statuettes, various objects of all sorts, owing nothing (or as little as possible) to the imitation of art that one can see in museums, salons and galleries; but that on the contrary appeal to humanity's first origins and the most spontaneous and personal invention.' Archives of the Collection de L' Art Brut, Lausanne.

Key features of Outsider Art included horror vacuii (the filling up of all the space on the drawing area), physiognomisation, intense and meticulous use of line, lack of differentiation and use of mixed media. A fascinating example of illustrated Outsider Art is the 15,145 page book The Story of the Vivian Girls, in what is known as the realms of the unreal, of the Glandeco-Angelinean war storm caused by the child slave rebellion. This was just one of the books written and illustrated by the reclusive and obsessive Henry Darger. The drawings created by primitive societies, the mentally ill, prisoners, folk artists and children influenced European avant-garde artists including Andre Masson (automatic drawing), Kandinsky (inspired by Folk Art), Jean Dubuffet, Paul Klee (inspired by graffiti and children's drawing) and Pablo Picasso (tribal masks). The anthology Der Blaue Reiter, published in Munich in 1912, included folk, tribal, naïve and children's work juxtaposed with work by artists such as Kandinsky and Matisse.

Explorations inspired by developments in psychoanalysis, and the role of ritual and intuition also informed the American Abstract Expressionist artists. Jackson Pollock (1912–1956) employed continuous drip lines on to his paintings in the late 1940s. These lines of paint dribbled, blotched and trickled over his canvases. The work of artists like Pollock, Klein and Calder influenced the graphic arts of the 1950s and 1960s. Abstract designs were echoed in the work of science fiction magazines and paperback illustrators and in the textile designs of graphic artists such as Lucienne Day and Ruth Adler. Pollock's rhythmic use of industrial paint was both gestural and controlled, intuitive, sensitive and determined. This controlled use of line and sensitive determination became fundamental in a new context in the mid-1970s onwards with graffiti and 'underground' urban street art.

THINKING VISUALLY: DRAWING

Client:
Liberty
Illustrator:
Andrew Foster
Title:
Window display

Related information

Related information such as historical precedents is included.

Additional information

Client, illustrator and image descriptions are included.

Illustrator Rob Ryan takes a break with his notebook at the ready and ...Eureka!

EUREKA! – VISUAL THINKING

The quest for intelligent, challenging, conceptually rigorous and meaningful illustration is a journey with no beginning or end. Learning is a lifelong activity. Being open and letting learning happen is the illustrator's first task.

Learning to think visually is a skill that must be practiced daily. As in sociology and anthropology, people and their socio-cultural context in the world are our subject matter. Being observant, listening, looking and participating in the world are necessary. The discipline of illustration has a vast and rich history. Contextualising one's work within and beyond that history is a way of establishing your own critical dialogue.

In order to communicate, elucidate, give insight to, and illuminate, the illustrator must be interested in humanity and in literature. Intellectual curiosity, hard work, ambition and passion are all essential, as is the ability to play and experiment. Ask the question, who will benefit from your work and what impact will it have on people? It is important to bring your own personality and concerns to a project. When asked what themes he explores in his work, contemporary illustrator Jon Burgerman replied: *'I like to mess around with simple word play and image associations in my work. Thematically ideas shift, depending on what the work is actually for. I like to inject cynicism, environmental concerns, puns, anxiety and saccharin sweetness where possible.'*

Analytical and intuitive skills are employed when generating a visual idea or concept. There are various methods for solving visual communication problems. When operating from a brief, rewrite the information in your own words to clarify it. Identify the audience, their concerns and cultural context. Research the client; establish the function of the project, the mood or tone of voice required, the context and media to be employed. Also, is the project worthwhile for you from an ethical point of view? It may be necessary to reject work if it compromises your ideals. Illustrations can be published in their thousands and will have an impact on the viewer; it is important to question in whose interest they are being produced and for what purpose.

The reality of working to project briefs, often solving others' problems while adhering to deadlines involves time management. Projects sometimes have to be researched, incubated, interpreted and responded to with imagination in a few hours and a strong work ethic is required. Spider diagrams, maps and word and image associations are aids often used by illustrators and designers to unlock creativity.

Brainstorm?

The search for successful concepts comes from generating lots of ideas. You could begin by listing every word you can think of analogous to your project then add images to these words.

Use dictionaries, a thesaurus, the internet, questionnaires, focus groups, sketchbooks, archives and primary and secondary research to expand ideas. At this stage of the brainstorming process every idea has potential.

Make combinations and links; give clichés or obvious solutions new twists. Techniques including metamorphosis, transformation, repetition, ambiguity, parody, simplification, addition, substitution, disguise, modification, *trompe l'oeil,* distortion, exaggeration, cropping, double entendre and decoration can be applied to your rough visuals.

Arthur Koestler stated in *The Act of Creation*, 1964, that 'the prerequisite of originality is the art of forgetting at the proper moment what we know'.

Being bold, honest and open to random juxtapositions of words and images will help you to reach that 'Eureka!' illumination moment and enable the solving of the problem with personal and original work that can entertain, engage, educate, provoke and inspire.

Generating many images helps refine and resolve compositional and conceptual issues. Before selecting images that are appropriate for the project, make sure all aspects of visual language have been fully explored.

Fundamental pictorial visual language elements include use of colour, texture, contrast, lighting, tonal values, shape, scale and size relationships, juxtaposition, perspective, concept hierarchy, balance, craft, overlap, use of line, composition and point of view.

All can alter the mood and atmosphere of the illustration. Metaphor, simile and synecdoche, metonym and syntax are linguistic concepts that can be employed in creating your own visual language.

The use of visual similes can also transform an illustration.

Client:
Illustrated Ape
Illustrator:
Andrew Rae
Title:
Perverted Science

A simile is *'a figure of speech involving the comparison of one thing with another thing of a different kind, used to make a description more emphatic or vivid.'* Oxford English Dictionary

'The thinking of the poet must habitually be tonality and cadence thinking, as with the artist it is colour, shape, image thinking. In each of these cases the discipline of the formulation is inseparable from the discipline of thinking itself.' Ben Shahn, The Shape of Content, 1957

Brainstorming

Below is a diagrammatic illustration by the author of a book entitled 'Interiors of the Subterraneans', which explores the youth tribes of London in the 1980s. The illustration was originally published in *i-D* magazine in 1984.

Research:

The systematic investigation into the study of materials and sources in order to establish facts and reach new conclusions.

Oxford English Dictionary

Illustrators are magpies, obsessive collectors, and always on the hunt for reference imagery. The search for imagery takes them to car boot sales, street markets, libraries, collector's fairs, jumble sales, charity shops and on to the internet.

Building a personal visual reference archive can take the form of plain chests full of ephemera, shelves packed with books and toys, and images filed away or websites digitally 'book marked'.

Being a cultural generalist is important for the illustrator and archives can be incredibly diverse, from Victorian engravings to 1930s mail order catalogues to 1960s annuals, records, stamps, film posters, comics, different types of papers, postcards, badges, skate company stickers, Japanese toys, and vinyl figures to 1970s punk fanzines.

Being aware of contemporary trends and theories in illustration, art and design is another aspect of research. It is important, however, not to limit oneself by imitating fashionable styles. Research should be broad and in-depth, enabling you to innovate, not imitate. It is also necessary to respond honestly to research material and be true to yourself.

For many illustrators the digital camera along with the sketchbook has become a new tool for importing masses of images straight to the computer. The illustrator's key digital tool, the scanner, is a fast way of processing research and creating project mood boards. Anything related to your project can be arranged on screen to stimulate idea development.

Illustrator Rian Hughes says he researches by *'sketching, thinking, reading… I feed as much information from various sources into my brain and then let it filter down to one elegant solution… I hope.'*

Jon Burgerman states that *'I'm not sure I actually switch into a research way of thinking, it's more of a continuous ongoing process involving keeping your eyes peeled at all times. For specific tasks I may go out to seek certain information. Google is a good lazy way of getting the ball rolling, though quite often the most interesting things are found away from the internet.'*

THINKING VISUALLY: EUREKA!

Here are a few examples of reference material from Wigan and NEW Studio archives.

Sketchbooks

The word 'sketch' sounds a little light and vague for what is the illustrator's essential daily tool. However, the sketchbook is the place where illustrators play with ideas: it is a personal space for exploring, collating, recording and juxtaposing images, also for reflecting and evaluating.

For illustrators the sketchbook can be the place where ideas are given form and refined. They can be purchased brand new in a wide range of sizes, weights of paper, colours and bindings. Alternatively second-hand books, blank books from printers or handmade and bound books containing various colours of paper can be used.

A primary use of the sketchbook is to reflect on personal progress and to act as an aid for future projects. Occasionally the free and vigorous approach of a sketchbook drawing might perfectly answer a project brief without further development.
It is useful to have a range of sizes of sketchbooks with separate functions. These can include a drawing book for visual notes from observation, memory or the imagination, a scrapbook and a pocket-sized visual diary.

The drawing book is used to experiment with mark making and drawing in various ways and media. Observational drawing extends visual language and when practised daily in a drawing book can build visual intelligence. All kinds of materials from biros, fibre and felt tips, pencils, graphite, pastels to watercolour washes, dip pens to charcoal can all be experimented with in the drawing book.

Examples of sketchbooks that demonstrate observational skills and capture the world with on-the-spot drawings are travel 'reportage' journals. Illustrators who have excelled in this area include Paul Hogarth, Edward Ardizzone, Paul Cox, Edward Bawden, David Gentleman, Edward Lear and Aude van Ryn. The giant of 20th-century art, Pablo Picasso, stated that he was a sketchbook! For further inspiration, reproductions of artists' sketchbooks can be investigated. Recommended are Leonardo da Vinci, Henry Moore, Albrecht Dürer, George Grosz, Egon Schiele and Jean Michel Basquiat.

Scrapbooks are visual archives of ephemera and found imagery that can be divided into categories or integrated into collages. All kinds of imagery can be pasted and

Client:
Finga-Thing
Illustrator:
Chris Drury
Description:
Development work

Artwork by Chris Drury : rat_tits@yahoo.com

fixed from photographs, postcards, photocopies, buttons and cloth to consumer packaging and printed matter. This can be arranged by texture or colour or themes such as body parts, buildings, vehicles, landscapes, animals, seascapes or maps.

Scrapbooks also fulfil a role as tools for contextual reflection and self-critical awareness. Promotional material including postcards, stickers, exhibition invitations and reviews can all be archived. In art and design education, sketchbooks and scrapbooks are essential evidence of a student's individual working processes. They are used as 'learning logs' or 'studio files' and demonstrate the student's visual thinking, level of experimentation, discovery and commitment.

Pocket-sized visual diaries are used to define thoughts, make notations and lists, record ideas and plan for new projects. Ideas can come at any time, e.g., on the bus, listening to music or watching television. Keeping a notebook close can help record that Eureka! illumination moment when it happens.

THINKING VISUALLY: SKETCHBOOKS

Inspirations

Inspirations and influences for illustrators are as diverse and as unique as their artwork. Here are a few influences, inspirations and an eclectic mix of concerns, themes and ideas from international illustrators.

The highly influential Saul Steinberg stated that – *'The whole history of art influenced me: Egyptian paintings, latrine drawings, primitive and insane art, Seurat, children's drawings, embroidery, Paul Klee…'*

1. Miles Donovan

'While at college in the mid '90s I didn't look to other illustrators for inspiration: there weren't many around I liked, and those I did like it was hard to actually see the work of because we didn't have the internet, so the people who influenced what I did then and do now are all dead painters (whatever I could lay my hands on in the library) – Basquiat, Warhol, Dubuffet.

'As for what inspires me now… Jamel Shabazz, Geoff McFetridge, Mike Mills, Michel Gondry, Spike Jonze, Saul Bass, M. Sasek, Jack Kirby, Blue Note covers, Rauschenberg.'

2. Dennis Eriksson

'Not so much other illustration. It can be other art forms like films from David Lynch, old diner menus, music by Kool Keith and Tav Falco, graphic design by Art Chantry, oil painting by Wayne Thiebaud, 19th-century lettering… a lot of things.'

3. Bill McConkey

'I'm very much old school. I follow mainly the American market of illustration, as it has some of the best illustrators working in a figurative and narrative manner…
I look more at traditional painters than any of the crop of digital artists around… everyone from Norman Rockwell to Brad Holland, Michael J. Deas, C. F. Payne, David Bowers, Donato Giancola… the list goes on and on.'

4. Sarah Jones

'Great accidents, the best things happen when I'm attempting something else – they move you on where you may not have gone otherwise. Good budgets always help oil the cogs! Finding beauty in banality is often a task I find myself attempting and that can inspire me.'

5. Paul Davis

'I can honestly say that pretty much everything influences me, positively, as well as negatively. I'm fundamentally against any kind of fundamentalism.'

LAST, MEAL

6. A. Richard Allen

'European comic books and classic illustration, conversation, drink, films, books, good TV.'

7. Elliot Thoburn

'Youth culture, films, fellow illustrators, some bloke on the bus, life in general really.'

8. Ian Pollock

'Drawing, raw drawing: illustration is published drawing.'

9. Peter Grundy

'The desire to create a personal visual language.'

10. Pedro Lino
'I always try to be aware of current issues such as social and political matters; I'm always watching and listening to the people on the streets, studying them. I'm also interested in a multitude of media, from graphic design, urban art to film, photography, typography – taking inspiration from it all.'

11. Louisa St. Pierre
'In my personal work, at the risk of sounding pretentious, I am interested in grand notions of humanity, spirituality and the meaning of life… Oh, and I'm a big fan of pandas; must try to include more of them in my work. Research? Internet, books, magazines, conversations with friends and colleagues, seminars… observing the world.'

12. Florence Manlik
'I don't know… It's all a bit abstract.'

13. Joanna Nelson
'The best word to describe my approach is eclectic. I am like a butterfly in that sense. The works of Matisse were important from the start, his use of colour and pattern, and I particularly like his later collage work where he literally cuts into colour in a remarkably knowing way. Also Paul Rand, Hannah Hoche, Matthew Richardson and Jan Lenica, Roman Cieslewicz (polish posters), David Hockney and Pablo Picasso.'

14. Kensuke Miyazaki
'American pop art, Japanese animation, haunted houses, amusement parks and Shinto shrines.'

15. Mick Brownfield
'Inspiration… after 36 busy years it's mainly the telephone, but I keep coming back to images from my early years… Comics,

THINKING VISUALLY: INSPIRATIONS

movies and ads: they really are my main inspiration and influence.'

16. eBoy
'Googling, blogs, films, books, shopping.'

17. Joel Lardner
'I am fascinated by sinister and beautiful imagery. I try to produce decorative pictures that convey a sense of menace or unease.'

18. Soner On
'I mainly discuss social issues I encounter in my native neighbourhood (Flatbush, Junction, Brooklyn, NYC). The customs, tongues and approach of Flatbush's inhabitants all play significant roles within my ideas.'

19. Serge Seidlitz
'Film, music, design, I travel, read comics, look at record covers, flyers, food packaging and obviously the people around me inspire me.'

20. Annabelle Hartmann
'*Day of the Dead*, tattoo art, customised motorcycles, surf culture, observations from my surroundings and places I have travelled, especially California.'

21. Boudicon
'Most of my research takes place internally, in my unconscious. It is the only library I can rely on because I want to make new work and not be too influenced by others. Sometimes it comes from other sources of media operating in the hip-hop or contemporary culture: books, videos, magazines, music, things overheard on the subway. But, ultimately, it's my unconscious where the research starts.'

22. Neil Webb
'Getting an income and fear of deadlines!

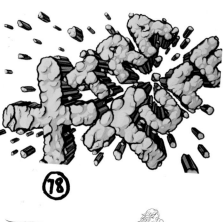

WWW.HARTMANNILLUSTRATION.COM

Generally not other illustration, but just about everything and anything else. Hard to narrow down influences as I think everybody's are unique, and deeply subconscious. Some stuff I particularly like at the moment includes Patrick Heron, late Ancient Greek vase figure painting, the band Hella, Alighiero Boetti, Cy Twombly, *Ghost in the Shell 2*, most things produced by the Neptunes – none of which is particularly evident in my work, which has to conform to its market in the end.'

23. Alex Williamson

'Books, literature and fiction, narrative and films. Much of my work is about trying to create narrative and capture a fictional moment in time – a film or novel within a single picture.

'Existential philosophy and points-of-view approach are at the root of most of my personal work and ideas. A range of other artists' work – Pop Art, Surrealism and Dadaism, particularly Magritte's painting 'The Menaced Assassin', Jeff Wall's photography, the work of early graphic designers Abram Games and Romek Marber – particularly the 1960s Penguin paper back covers.

'Also 1960s/70s Polish and East European/Soviet graphic posters. Urban landscapes – cities, people, concrete, flyovers, tower blocks, layers of texture, narrative and meaning.'

24. Simon Pemberton

'My main influence has always been texture: I used to draw it obsessively, then moved on to building 3D constructions/collages from huge collections of found objects and textures and I now scan/photograph or paint them. That and a contradictory love of empty space and minimalism.'

THINKING VISUALLY: INSPIRATIONS

Observational drawing from the recent sketchbook of the Urban artist known as *PMH.*

DRAWING – THE PROCESS OF DRAWING

Drawing is a process of preparation leading to completion in another media; it is also a discipline and a form of visual art in its own right. Illustration combines convincing drawing with imagination, ideas and content.

For the illustrator, drawing is a fundamental visual thinking tool.

Points of view on the value of drawing vary greatly. For example, some feel that life drawing is not an essential skill, but the majority of illustrators interviewed around the world for this book felt that it was vital.

The illustrator and type designer Rian Hughes said *'there is no substitute for a fearsome grasp of anatomy, perspective and composition; only when you have learnt to master the technical aspects can you successfully express yourself.'*

Drawing enables us to interpret the world graphically, as well as invent imaginary worlds of our own. A complex and multifunctional activity, drawing makes our thoughts visible and visually articulates ideas and emotions.

The complex process of drawing involves looking, seeing, responding, improvising, feeling, discovering, negotiating, designing, reasoning, enquiring, translating, scrutinising, ordering, mapping, objectifying, exploring, measuring, documenting and communicating. When asked what inspired him, illustrator Ian Pollock said *'drawing, raw drawing: illustration is published drawing'*.

By exploring the edges of the discipline of drawing, illustrators can extend their visual vocabulary. Diverse methods and media from the traditional to leading-edge technologies can be applied in a range of contexts. Cognitive, improvisatory, gestural and kinetic processes can be explored with drawing.

Approaches can include drawing as trace, performance, writing, sound and as object. The activity of drawing can take place in many environments, including live and virtual, analogue and digital, architectural, interactive and the reactive.

By researching a broad canon of artists, illustrators, designers and animators we can explore the influence of representational conventions

The Timeline
Drawing has played a fundamental role throughout the history of the human race.

The earliest surviving examples of this ancient art form can be found in Lascaux, France and Altamira, Spain (see opposite, courtesy of Deutsches Museum). These cave drawings date from c. 12,000 BC. Pre-dating written language, the exact function of these sophisticated drawings remains a mystery. Although their purpose could be religious or ritualistic, these hunting scenes demonstrate the primal need to communicate and to draw from life. Stylised conventions have always been employed in drawing.

The ancient Egyptian hieroglyphics integrated phonetic and pictographic signs with both abstract and observational drawing. Colour was used symbolically, heads were depicted in profile, torsos were viewed from the front and legs in three-quarter view (examples include illustrated scrolls such as the *Book of the Dead* and the *Ramesseum Papyrus*). Symbolic conventions are evident in the diagrammatic drawing of Mesopotamia and in the use of space, colour and visual hierarchy in Islamic art.

In China and Japan drawing was executed with fluid calligraphic brush work. The Greeks and Romans introduced technical illustration and new ideas, such as proportion and perspective. Papyrus scrolls were gradually replaced by vellum and the introduction of the codex in the first century AD. Religious worship continued to inform drawing with the illumination of sacred religious texts, such as *The Book of Kells* from 8th century AD, Ireland. Classical ideas were renewed during the Renaissance in Italy and an intellectual exploration of the arts and sciences placed man at the centre of the universe. Renaissance ideas and values spread throughout Europe from Italy. Drawing systems and machines, and studies of anatomy, proportion, geometry and composition were introduced and developed. The drawings of the artist/illustrators Leonardo da Vinci (1452–1519), Michelangelo (1475–1519), Raphael (1483–1520), Holbein (1497–1543) and Albrecht Dürer (1471–1528) exemplify the imaginative use of line, tone and observational clarity.

The Renaissance approach to drawing led to the establishment of academies and has been central to the education of artists in the West for centuries. Alternative approaches unleashed by the Renaissance include the highly imaginative work of Hieronymous Bosch (1450–1516), Pieter Brueghel the Elder (1520–1569) and Jacques Callot (1592–1635). They took inspiration from medieval folk art, narrative, storytelling and social commentary. Illustration, a new highly personal and imaginative tradition in drawing, began. Drawing exists within traditions, representational conventions, a culture, a geographical location and a time in history. By engaging in semiotic and contextual analysis of drawing we can examine how social, ideological, political, ritual, religious, symbolic, economic, aesthetic, communicative and technological factors have affected

its creation, form and function. The interpretive line carries many connotations – spontaneous, expressive, versatile, dynamic, subtle, immediate and personal. It is this primal quality that has led to the search for inspiration in the primitive, the irrational and the shamanistic. This search for the 'other' the 'authentic', the primal original artistic mind and the desire to 'unlearn' is evident in the philosophy of Paul Klee (1879–1940): *'I want to be as though newborn, knowing absolutely nothing about Europe; ignoring facts and fashions, to be almost primitive.'*

Anne Howeson

An example of drawing from memory, part of a series of personal work.

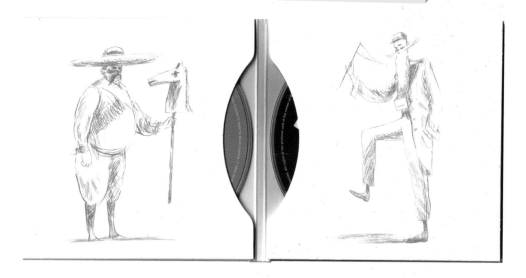

Client:
Elbow
Illustrator:
Michael O'Shaughnessy
Title:
Record sleeves

Michael O'Shaughnessy

'Drawing is fundamental to the fabric of illustration. Once you have changed many of the perceived notions of 'what drawing is'… you can get on with the task of exploring a visual language. Our answers are found in manipulating a chosen medium; they can often start with a pencil and piece of paper. Drawing the world around us lets us see the world.'

Outsider Art
Idiosyncratic, magical and obsessive, Visionary, Folk and Outsider Art have proven to be a powerful influence on the development of art and illustration.

Historical precedents include the imaginative works of Arcimboldo, Bomarzo, Goya and Bosch. The visionary tradition of naïve and obsessive art continued with Henri Rousseau, Morris Hirschfield, Ferdinand Cheval, Simon Rodia, Madge Gill, Adolf Wölfli, Henry Darger and Howard Finster. In 1945, Jean Dubuffet invented the term 'Art Brut' to describe *'artistic works such as paintings, drawings, statues and statuettes, various objects of all sorts, owing nothing (or as little as possible) to the imitation of art that one can see in museums, salons and galleries; but that on the contrary appeal to humanity's first origins and the most spontaneous and personal invention.'* Archives of the Collection de L' Art Brut, Lausanne.

Key features of Outsider Art included *horror vacuii* (the filling up of all the space on the drawing area), physiognomisation, intense and meticulous use of line, lack of differentiation and use of mixed media. A fascinating example of illustrated Outsider Art is the 15,145 page book *The Story of the Vivian Girls, in what is known as the realms of the unreal, of the Glandeco-Angellinean war storm caused by the child slave rebellion*. This was just one of the books written and illustrated by the reclusive and obsessive Henry Darger. The drawings created by primitive societies, the mentally ill, prisoners, folk artists and children influenced European avant-garde artists including Andre Masson (automatic drawing), Kandinsky (inspired by Folk Art), Jean Dubuffet, Paul Klee (inspired by graffiti and children's drawing) and Pablo Picasso (tribal masks). The anthology *Der Blaue Reiter,* published in Munich in 1912, included folk, tribal, naïve and children's work juxtaposed with work by artists such as Kandinsky and Matisse.

Explorations inspired by developments in psychoanalysis, and the role of ritual and intuition also informed the American Abstract Expressionist artists. Jackson Pollock (1912–1956) employed continuous drip lines on to his paintings in the late 1940s. These lines of paint dribbled, blotched and trickled over his canvases. The work of artists like Pollock, Klein and Calder influenced the graphic arts of the 1950s and 1960s. Abstract designs were echoed in the work of science fiction magazines and paperback illustrators and in the textile designs of graphic artists such as Lucienne Day and Ruth Adler. Pollock's rhythmic use of industrial paint was both gestural and controlled, intuitive, sensitive and determined. This controlled use of line and sensitive determination became fundamental in a new context in the mid-1970s onwards with graffiti and 'underground' urban street art.

Client:
Liberty

Illustrator:
Andrew Foster

Title:
Window display

The Portrait

The portrait is a core genre of the fine art tradition and a key theme in the practice of professional illustration. In the novel *The Picture of Dorian Gray* (1891), Oscar Wilde wrote that *'every portrait painted with feeling is a portrait of the artist, not the sitter.'*

From sarcophagi to statues, coins to paintings and miniatures to murals, portraiture is the attempt to represent a likeness of someone so as to create an illusion of a face. Portraits can also be expressive and/or abstract. These representations of people cannot be removed from their social, political, historical and cultural contexts. Portraits also function as a visual memory of the artist, the subject painted and a moment in time.

The representation of a person's character and personality involves the artist's interpretation and point of view. When researching portraiture, ask what impression does the sitter want to project and to what extent has the artist enhanced or undermined this.

It is necessary to question the function of the portrait, why it was commissioned and who it was intended for. Is it a form, for example, of self-promotion or a comment on status or religious belief?

Within the present image-saturated post-modern cultural paradigm, portraiture's key concepts such as identity, representation, gender, status and power are uncertain, ambiguous and fragmenting. The expressions of the face can suggest a wide variety of feelings and emotions.

An exercise in drawing a portrait could involve capturing a range of facial expressions that signify emotions such as sadness, disdain, surprise, devotion, anxiety, fear, joy, embarrassment, anger, loneliness, contentment, puzzlement, boredom, ecstasy, determination.

Changing the direction of lighting can significantly alter the mood and atmosphere of the portrait. Draw the face from a range of positions and note the effect each position

THINKING VISUALLY: DRAWING

Client:
Personal work
Illustrator:
Miles Donovan
Title:
CMYK Boy

(Right) Woody
and (left) Boy George
by Nigel Robinson.

(Below) Mekon's sleeves
by Stephen Bliss.

Happy talk

The answer to our constant pursuit of happiness
may be right under our noses. Lucienne Roberts
looks at the benefits of some 'quality distraction'.

has on the emotion you are trying to convey. Employ colour to also enhance emotions. Concentrate on the relationships between the key features of the face such as the eyes, hair, neck, skin, mouth, forehead, nose, cheeks, jaw and teeth.

In a project addressing the construction of images, illustration students were set a project on self-portraiture. Visual research for this project included the historical contextualisation of this genre, analysing notions of status, self-worth, psyche, gender, wealth, vanity and identity. The visual construction of self-portraits and the manipulation of pictorial properties in relation to the portrait's intended meaning were explored. The self-portrait project also involved students depicting themselves in an historical context and in an appropriate media.

Students' projects were diverse and inventive, finished work included the construction of interpretations of ancient Egyptian sarcophagi (from casting the whole body) to self-portraits as in the workers of the 1920s London Docklands. Other themes ranged from aristocratic self-portraits, from the era of Marie Antoinette, to the Dublin uprising of Easter 1916.

An eclectic range of artists who have created portraits in a range of media were also introduced to the students, including Peter Blake (his 'Self-portrait with Badges'), Andy Warhol (Marilyn Monroe prints), Shepard Fairey ('Obey Giant'), Cindy Sherman (self-portraits), Paul Cézanne, Rembrandt (self-portraits at different stages of his life), Max Beckmann, Pablo Picasso (Cubism), Hanoch Piven (mixed media), Alberto Giacometti (abstraction), Guiseppe Arcimboldo, Hiromix (photography), Leigh Bowery (performance), Jenny Saville, Francis Bacon (distortion), Egon Schiele, Frida Kahlo (Surrealism), Chuck Close, Mariko Mori, Stanley Spencer, Vincent van Gogh, Amedeo Modigliani, Albrecht Dürer ('Portrait of a Young Man'), Marlene Dumas and Leonardo da Vinci (Mona Lisa).

Ian Law (left)

'This piece came from a body of work based on the plight of the Hood Hut Howl, a small fictional community struggling to recover from the fall-out of failing industry. These portraits are of the inhabitants who still remain in the area, isolated and unable to leave.

'For me portraiture is a vehicle in which an emotion or situation can be expressed simply within a human-like form. I work without reference and rarely draw from life, as I feel the physical act of mark making should remain free, intuitive and uninterrupted by outside stimuli.

'This mixture of memory and physicality presents the viewer with an unreal reality, a projected form in which a real emotion is embedded. The early work of George Baselitz, Jean Dubuffet and Cy Twombly has informed my working methods, while the films of Werner Herzog provided examples of isolation within communities.'

THINKING VISUALLY: PORTRAITURE

'If' Is The Middle Word In Life

There may not be any set rules on life drawing, but there is a number of helpful fundamental techniques. Begin by finding an interesting position to view the model from, then start looking and measuring. At this analytical stage, closing an eye and holding up a pencil to measure can help. Compare and look at proportions while making a few marks. While scanning and cross-referencing put in the directional and structural lines of the figure. Indicating a frame around the figure can help judge the relationships and proportions. It is important to look for the rhythm of the figure in space.

Observe horizontal and vertical angles and axes, and employ your imagination and intuition. Be aware of internal structure and the three-dimensional volume of the figure (light cross-section lines can help). The activity of drawing the figure involves the co-ordination of eye, brain and hand. The processes of all three should alternate and respond to the information that is being captured visually. The combination of contour line and tone indicates volume and weight. Look for and describe shadow, light, form, tone, balance, foreshortening for depth, movement, posture, negative and positive space, tensions and gesture.

Note

For further study of life drawing, research the drawings of Paul Cézanne, Michelangelo, Titian, Gauguin, Leonardo da Vinci, Edward Degas, Egon Schiele, Albrecht Dürer, Amedeo Modigliani, Kirchner, Ingres, Diego Velázquez and Picasso.

This image is from a one-day Masquerade project.

Mask by
Nadezda Lantuka

PLAYTIME – WORKING PROCESSES

'I paint objects as I think them not as I see them.' Pablo Picasso, 1959

Illustrators generally work to set briefs – a visual problem – which they solve by communicating an idea; the idea may be executed in a wide variety of ways, from the emotionally charged to the whimsical. Every illustrator has a working process. The illustrator employs skill and imagination, original ways of thinking and making, sourcing, navigating and manipulating techniques, methods, technologies and tools.

There is no formula for illustration; it is a matter of finding your own vision and being honest with yourself. Experimentation enables the illustrator to rethink, reinvent and rediscover a unique personal vision. While working to solve others' visual problems, the most interesting illustrators draw on their own interests and curiosity. The most vital work transcends and challenges the clichés and limitations of fashionable conventions and orthodoxy.

Picture making involves play and experimentation with ideas, form, colour and composition, and with contexts and content. The resourceful illustrator uses a multidisciplinary toolbox to generate ideas and select, edit, test and develop processes and materials. Constant change impacts on all forms of visual communication: a flexibility of approach and emphasis on critical thinking, idea generation and fundamental drawing skills are paramount. New technology should be engaged with critically and imaginatively, and alternative methods and techniques investigated.

Longevity as an illustrator comes from originality of approach and developing a personal creative visual language, also from an understanding of the professional and industrial practices, and processes of illustration.

International, accomplished, versatile and professional illustrators were asked to comment on their working processes and an interesting picture of early 21st-century practice emerges. Play and experimentation have central roles as illustrators generate ideas and visualise in a broad range of new and traditional technologies and media.

In a one-day project called Masquerade (a homage to Saul Steinberg), first-year illustration students explored Representation, Cultural Identity, Gender and Race, responding visually to the question 'What

Neil Webb

'A lot of thinking, rough sketches, then photographic reference taken to the computer.'

Paul Davis

'Notebook after notebook after notebook because I feel sick when I forget potentially good ideas. I don't slack. I take photographs. I draw. I scan. I Photoshop.'

Rian Hughes

'Inspiration is drawn from many sources, and it's a different route for each job. The job itself has to have some kind of internal logic and structure, both conceptually and visually. This harmonic whole is teased into shape via a refining process, from basic blocked-in colours to final addition of texture and shadow.'

Ian Pollock

'Pencil (thoughts), ink for decision. White sheet of paper for clear mind. State of stillness.'

A. Richard Allen

'Sketchbooks, ideas, buffing roughs on Photoshop, finished line work with brush and ink, scanned colours applied on Photoshop.'

Alex Williamson

'Collage/montage: I use photocopies, drawing, cut out, photocopies, drawings, cut-out photography and found ephemera to create a collaged image. I have an ever-evolving collection of random graphic ephemera, shapes, textures and images from which I often work. I am interested in juxtaposition and random accident, creating a new image from existing or separately created elements. I was originally a printmaker (silkscreen) and this process has informed the way I work now in digital media.'

Dennis Eriksson

'I work fast but I do the same picture over and over. I repeat the procedure until I'm satisfied. If I run out of ideas I usually fill a whole table with drawing I've done that I'm satisfied with, and just stare at them for an hour. To get the right feeling I try not to stick with my first idea. It's important to rethink. But if I have a good concept I will redraw it until it works, not skip to a new idea after only one try.'

Florence Manlik

'I don't think, I draw: some accident happens and the drawing builds up to save the disaster. Sometimes it succeeds and sometimes it fails.'

Elliot Thoburn

'Research ideas, mock-up final proof.'

Simon Pemberton

'My final product is digital, but I also draw, paint, take photos and collect collage elements off computer and scan them in. I draw back into the work on computer too and manipulate my own drawing and painting. Initial ideas are just scribbled, but compositions are often worked out that way and they look scarily like the final thing sometimes.'

Sarah Jones
'It usually starts with walking around my house looking in books, followed by a cup of tea. Then some shambolic fumbling with roller printing ink and scanner. Lastly an attempt to orchestrate everything on computer.'

Bill McConkey
'Every job starts obviously with the brief. I'll email or phone the client once I've had a read through to discuss any details not already outlined. The next step for me is to sketch up a little thumbnail, which I usually do on lined paper as I don't want to be precious at this point. The next thing is a rough. I send a thumbnail doodle showing composition and the main elements. I blow up the thumbnail to working size and use it as an under-drawing. I then work out all the details on screen and edit where I need to edit. I hate being restricted by a tightly rendered pencil drawing at such an early part of the process. I like to feel my way through the final work intuitively.'

Chris Drury
'After a good few weeks of listening and doodling I start to collage all of my ideas, seeing which elements work well with each other, cut and paste style. From here I begin to make more finished biro drawings, which are all scanned, coloured and arranged in Freehand.'

eBoy
'You could call it rotation… one starts defining the basics like the grid or the resolution, then the next eBoy and so on. This could last some weeks or months depending on the amount of pixels. Rotation prevents boredom and results in rich, layered work.'

Mick Brownfield
'My working process is to receive a job, discuss the brief and the deadline and the fee. I then ask for an order and begin pencil roughs, which I will email to the client. On approval I will think about which style and technique is suitable. I then complete the illustration and make sure the client receives it on deadline, but not before.'

Peter Grundy
'Client project: research/discussion/thinking/idea/creation. Personal work: idea/creation.'

Peter Gudynas
'Before 1987 the main body of my work was produced by photomontage and airbrush techniques. Since then I have explored the creative potential of electronic media and computer image manipulation: between 1986–1990 Olivetti PC computer, 8-bit Pluto graphics controller and 2D designer Point software. After 1990 to the present involved using Apple Macintosh computers 8500, G3, G4, G5 with Photoshop, Illustrator and 3D-modelling software. I work out ideas as drawings on paper, thumbnail sketches develop an idea and composition, working with source material where needed. Once I have the basis of something to go on I will start work on the computer and set up any photographic materials and traditional artwork required for scanning.'

WHY AM I HERE? WHY ARE ANY OF US HERE?

WHAT DOES ANY OF THIS ACTUALLY <u>MEAN?</u>

Everything seems so utterly pointless...

I DON'T EVEN KNOW WHAT TO THINK ANYMORE...

I CAN BARELY BREATHE FOR ALL THE WORRY.

MY JACKET LOOKS SILLY

I FEEL SICK PRETTY MUCH ALL OF THE TIME. OH GOD! <u>SWEET</u> <u>MERCY!</u> WHAT AM I (DOING) WITH MY LIFE? IT'S ALWAYS THE SAME: A BIT SHIT. I AM A SORRY SHADOW OF MY FORMER SELF

Things you thought today

Title:
"Your Thoughts"
by Al Murphy

WOW! YOU LOOK REALLY GOOD!
YOU WERE SO FUNNY TODAY!
I LOVED WHAT YOU HAD TO OFFER
TO ALL OF THIS... UTTERLY <u>AMAZING</u>

EVERYBODY LIKES YOUR NEW JACKET
YOU LOOK NICE IN IT ████████

YOU PUT A REALLY GOOD TURN
IN THERE. I CAN'T BELIEVE YOU
DID ALL OF THIS YOURSELF
HOW DO YOU MANAGE IT?

GREAT I heard that ██
REALLY likes your face.
I THINK ██ MIGHT WANT TO GET WITH
YOU TONIGHT. YOU SHOULD GET WITH
██ YOU COULD GO ALL THE WAY.
BRILLIANT. Just FANTASTIC

Things other people thought today

RESCUE

THINKING VISUALLY: WORKING PROCESSES

Experimental Workshop

The images below and on the following pages show Mark Pawson at work: a collector, producer and distributor of a wide range of work from artists' books, postcards, badges, multiples, t-shirts and postcards, and for many years a member of the international mail-art network.

1. Printing

He says he likes to 'own the means of production'. Pawson's house is a library, museum and resource centre where he always has several projects on the go in overlapping development.

He describes his working process as: *'A continual, impulsive, unfocused process of filtering, sorting out, editing, grouping, forgetting, remembering ideas, themes, materials…'*

Mark Pawson

'From ideas sketched out and scribbled down in writing pads and on Post-it® notes, certain ideas will come to the front, others drop away, then I figure out if it's best suited to be presented as a book/card/badge/whatever, and the most appropriate formats/production methods – make dummy versions, which sit around the room for ages, gathering annotated notes and suggestions. Decide how many to make, make them, price them, sell them, distribute them.'

2. Badge making

3. Stamping

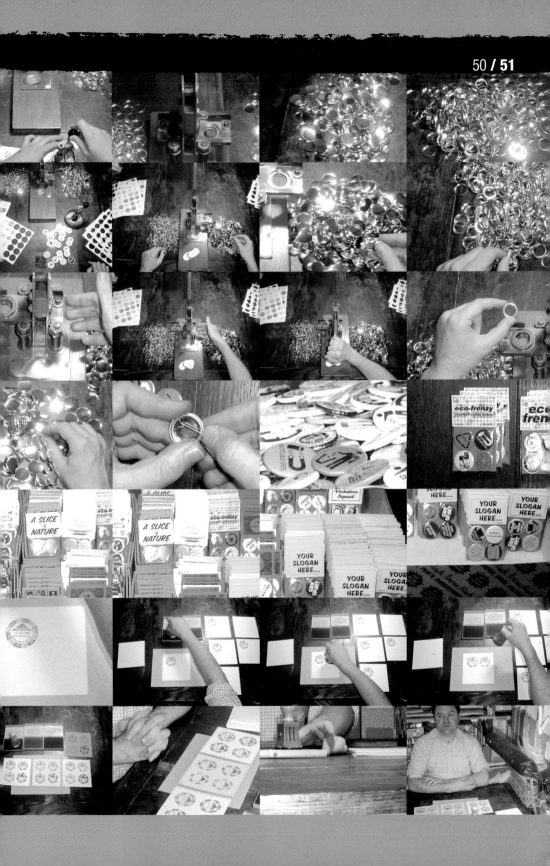

Cross-media and Cultural Cut-ups
Three words that have had a significant cultural impact on image-making are:

Collage – *Origin: early 20th century from French, literally meaning 'gluing' – a form of art in which various materials such as photographs and pieces of paper or fabric are arranged and stuck to a backing.*

Montage – *Origin: early 20th-century France, from 'monter' – to mount – the technique of selecting, editing and piecing together separate sections of film to form a continuous whole new composite. From fragments of pictures, text or music.*

Assemblage – *A machine or object made of pieces fitted together. A work of art made by grouping together found or unrelated objects.*

(Oxford English Dictionary)

People have always collected, edited and assembled found materials for communicative, ritual and decorative purposes. Ancient civilisations, primitive and contemporary tribal societies have used collage to adorn their bodies, masks, costumes and jewellery.

THINKING VISUALLY: PLAYTIME

This photograph was taken at Chris Draper's studio and shows the objects he uses in his collages.

Origins

Techniques for creating mosaics developed by the Babylonians and Egyptians were used extensively by the Roman and Byzantine civilisations. In Asia the use of collage began with the invention of paper, many examples being found in Chinese and

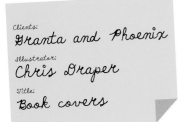

Clients:
Granta and Phoenix
Illustrator:
Chris Draper
Title:
Book covers

Japanese scrolls and collage poems. In Europe from the 15th century onwards religious iconography became the source material for collaged panels and greetings cards. During the 16th century, Dutch and Flemish painters developed the *trompe l'oeil*, the 'fooling of the eye' school.

The Industrial Revolution

The Industrial Revolution, with its technological advances, created masses of printed graphic illustration, leading to the popular use of collage during the Victorian era. The invention of photography in 1839 (daguerreotype), an interest in Primitive Art and social and political upheaval would lead to collage's widespread use by the Avant-Garde Art movements.

The Avant-Garde

The Cubist works of Picasso, Braque and Juan Gris involved pasting and fixing newspaper, wallpaper, cloth, wood, sand and metal on to paintings and reliefs. Assemblage (bringing together) has fuelled art and design ever since. Key figures include Futurist Umberto Boccioni, who incorporated newsprint on to his paintings and sculptures, and Dadaists Raoul Hausmann and Marcel Duchamp (the inventor of the 'Readymade'). For John Heartfield, George Grosz and Hannah Hoche, photomontage became a powerful weapon to satirise social and political issues. The juxtaposition and mixing of images led to a metamorphosis, which Raoul Hausmann described as 'a vision that is optically and conceptually new'. Perhaps one of the most innovative artists using collage was Kurt Schwitters, who described his massive output of collages and constructions as MERZ (a word he cut out of an advertising poster for Hanover's Kommerz-und Privatbank and glued into one of his collages). Another collage technique known as 'Papier Colle' – the pasting of coloured paper – can be seen in the work of Henri Matisse, Ben Nicholson and Victor Passmore.
'To cut freely into a colour reminds me of direct carving by sculptures.'
Henri Matisse, Jazz, 1947

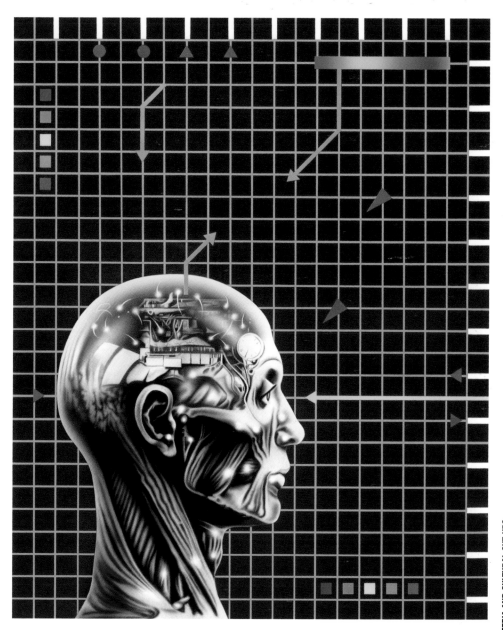

Techno Surrealism

Featured above is the work of digital artist, Peter Gudynas. His work is described as 'montages in part related to the Surrealist lineage that stretches from Bosch through Dali, Ernst and Paolozzi. However, they represent a new "Techno Surrealist" practice that responds to our contemporary unreality. A seductive and intense mixture that encourages our own enquiry into the consequences of our irresistible reach for the future.' Stephen Pochin, Retrovision: Posthuman Photofictions (Coningsby Gallery exhibition catalogue), 1999

THINKING VISUALLY: CROSS-MEDIA AND CULTURAL CUT-UPS

The use of collage and montage was also in evidence in the experimental films of the Avant-Garde artists such as Hans Richter, Oskar Fischinger, Léger, Buñuel and Dali. The powerful montage narrative and documentary films of Eisenstein and Vertov also combined social comment with experimentation.

The dynamic use of photomontage in political posters and Agitprop art was important to the Russian artists of the 1920s. Key exponents were El Lissitzky, Rodchenko and László Moholy-Nagy. The medium was also explored further at the Bauhaus in Weimar and in Berlin, where teaching methods promoted abstract design and original use of materials.

The Modernist ethos of the Bauhaus, Constructivism and De Stijl would be assimilated by illustrators and graphic designers, the styles of Modernist photomontage repeatedly appropriated to endorse products to this day.

The Surreal

Surrealism, with its preoccupation with the subconscious and fantasy, extended the use of collage further. Key artists included Max Ernst (a collagist who also invented frottage – a process of taking a rubbing from an uneven surface), Magritte (hand-painted collage), Man Ray (inventor of Rayogram images) and the maverick collagist and maker of three-dimensional constructions, Joseph Cornell. Surrealism would go on to influence new art forms, as well as the applied arts, illustration, graphic design and advertising.

In turn mass-produced commercial imagery would again influence the art world. The use of collage was widespread in Pop Art during the 1950s and 1960s. Of note are the works of Eduardo Paolozzi, Peter Blake, Andy Warhol, Robert Rauschenberg, Richard Hamilton and Niki de Saint Phalle.

Neo-Dada

Neo-Dada movements such as Fluxus and later Punk, including the graphic work of Jamie Reid, Malcolm Garrett and Russell Mills, continued this anarchic cut-up tradition.

Post-modernism is a self-conscious use of earlier styles and conventions. This eclectic mixing of media and departure from Modernism has informed commercial and fine art, architecture and criticism. Post-modern artists, illustrators and designers have embraced the use of colour photocopiers, scanners, digital cameras, computers and software applications such as Photoshop. Contemporary image-makers create compositions using both traditional and digital tools, leaving room for serendipity (events occurring by chance).

Title:
The Tempest, Sycorax

Illustrator:
Janet Woolley

Description:
Personal work

Illustrators inspired by artwork such as Kurt Schwitter's Merzbau, Joseph Cornell's boxes, Oldenburg's soft sculptures, Calder's mobiles, Jan Svankmeyer's films, as well as by Outsider, Visionary and Folk Art, also substitute the second for the third dimension.

To this kind of illustrator, feathers, toys, wire, thread, sand, nails, driftwood, felt, cloth, beads, pebbles, matchboxes, shells and all kinds of flotsam and jetsam have a magical ingredient when combined to communicate ideas and emotions.

Peter Gudynas

Techno Surrealist Peter Gudynas has over the past 28 years achieved a reputation as a graphic artist, illustrator and photographer in the UK, USA and Europe.

He states that: 'Collage, as an artistic practice, has been an important technique and resurfaces in my work as ideas, images and symbols juxtaposed in time and space. Collage with its links to Dada provides a philosophy of diversity that weaves or fragments the past and present and as arch Post-modern writer William Burroughs has said, may allow hints of the future to seep through. With computer manipulation of the photograph and image, a new area of creative practice has been further opened up, redefining and extending the possibilities and infusing the technique with a new aesthetic dynamism and potential.'

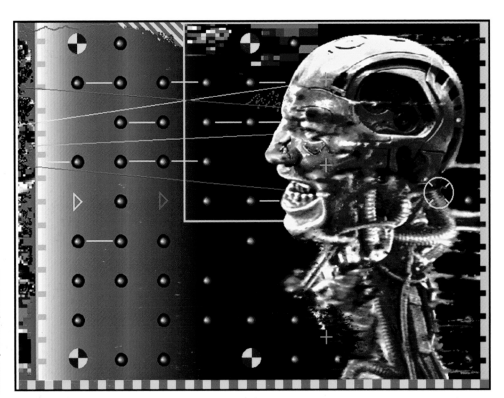

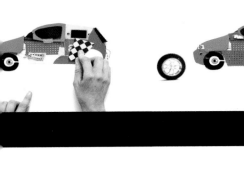

Client:
Toyota Echo Cars

Illustrator:
Marie O'Connor

Title:
Animated collage

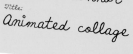

POINTS OF VIEW – CARICATURE

In *Nicholas Nickleby,* Charles Dickens wrote that 'there are only two styles of portrait painting: the serious and the smirk.'

Caricature is the distortion or exaggeration of a person's most striking features: a likeness to the person has to remain, but our perception of the individual changes. The word caricature is derived from the Italian word 'caricare', to 'load or surcharge'.

The purpose of caricature is to hold a person to ridicule through humour and satire. It makes use of polemic to offend. The technique employs physiognomics, whereby a person's facial features or expression indicates their personality or character, mood and emotion. Caricatures became fashionable in the 18th century and Francis Grose published his *Rules for Drawing Caricatures* in 1788. During the 19th century the publishing of caricature increased with the rise in circulation of periodicals such as *Le Charivari* and *Punch.* In 1845 Rodolphe Töpffer (credited with inventing the comic book) wrote *Essai de Physiognomie,* in which he illustrated how facial features could be exaggerated for fun, satire and mockery.

The English engraver, portrait and history painter William Hogarth is recognised as highly influential in this field. He observed and commented on social injustice, vice, luxury and hypocrisy and shocked society in England. His key works include 'The Rake's Progress', 'Industry and Idleness', 'Marriage à la Mode' and 'The Harlot's Progress'. England has always been famous for its satire and caricaturists, from Hogarth to George Cruikshank to Thomas Rowlandson, James Gillray to David Low, Ronald Searle to Ralph Steadman, Gerald Scarfe, Fluck and Law to Steve Bell and Martin Rowson.

The tradition is also strong in France; in 1834 caricaturist Charles Philipon drew the satirical 'Les Poires' illustration of King Louis Philippe transforming into a pear and because of this, his paper *Le Charivari* was heavily fined. Honoré Daumier who worked for *La Caricature* was imprisoned for five months for another visual attack on the King. Political portrait caricature reached a new raw intensity in Germany during the Weimar Republic with the work of Berlin Dadaists George Grosz and John Heartfield.

Grosz's drawings of corruption, decadence, war veterans, poverty and fear appeared in Malik Verlag journals such as *Die Pleite* and *Der Knüppel.* Of his work Grosz said *'I got rid of my burning hatred in drawings', (A Little Yes and a Big No,* 1955). Heartfield's many

collaged caricatures visually attacked the rise of the Nazis, including showing Hitler with a spine of Deutschmarks and portraying Goebbels as a Hyena. Witty and satirical attacks on injustice, corruption and vanity, targeting politicians, celebrities, clerics, dictators and royalty etc., have led to some remarkable and iconic images and continue to be a feature of our visual culture. The young political cartoonist has a rich history of predecessors from which to draw inspiration and with an interest in current affairs many targets to aim at. There are many caricaturists worldwide creating conceptually rigorous, humorous and powerful illustration. Old traditional print media is being superseded by new media impacting on the dissemination of illustration. Some publications are choosing not to risk publishing political caricatures for fear of causing offence. However, some still publish outstanding work such as Steve Bell's work for the *Guardian* and Steve Brodner's caricatures in the *New Yorker*. Also there are new opportunities to produce work on websites and in animation and for television.

In order to research this area of graphic satire, polemic and metaphor, look at the work of William Hogarth, George Cruikshank, Thomas Rowlandson, Honoré Daumier, James Gillray, Sir John Tenniel, Théophile Alexandre Steinlen, André Gill, Thomas Nast, David Low, Olaf Gulbransson, George Grosz, John Heartfield, Ben Shahn, David Levine, Ralph Steadman, Gerald Scarfe, Ronald Searle, Brad Holland, Steve Brodner, Edward Sorel, Peter Fluck and Roger Law (*Spitting Image*), Steve Bell and Martin Rowson.

Tommy Cooper
and
Chariot (left)
by

Ian Pollock

THINKING VISUALLY: CARICATURE

The Decorative

During the 1960s and 1970s new markets opened up for illustration; fashion, advertising, design, the music industry and publishing with its children's books, new magazines, cards, posters, paperbacks and gifts all expanded quickly.

The ornate and decorative illustration of the time drew inspiration from William Morris and the late 19th-century Arts and Crafts Movement. Morris's company Morris, Marshall, Faulkner & Co., designed and made their own products such as wallpaper, tiles, tapestries and books. In the 1960s this multi-disciplinary approach combined eclectic influences such as Victoriana, Rococo, Art Nouveau and Surrealism, and the work of Dulac, Mucha and Toulouse-Lautrec.

A key text for graphic artists was *The Grammar of Ornament* by Owen Jones (1856), featuring colourful chromolithography illustrations of ornamentation from around the world. The English illustrator Aubrey Beardsley (1872–1898) was a major influence on the illustration of the 1960s and 1970s, and continues to inspire today.

Beardsley's sinuous and elegant use of line and mannered black-and-white compositions represented the *fin de siècle* decadence of its day. These works include illustrations for Oscar Wilde's *Salomé* and his drawings for Mademoiselle de Maupin, Volpone, Lysistrata and the Rape of the Lock. Beardsley worked in a number of styles, drawing inspiration from pre-Raphaelite and Japanese art; his drawings featured small faces, elongated figures and rich ornamentation. Beardsley set trends with his contributions to the *Yellow Book*, an illustrated quarterly that featured pictures that did not illustrate the text demonstrating the art for art's sake attitude of the *fin de siècle*.

Leading illustrators of the 1960s include Alan Aldridge, famous for his *The Beatles Illustrated Lyrics*, *The Butterfly Ball and the Grasshopper's Feast* and poster design for Andy Warhol's *Chelsea Girls* (1968). Rick Griffin's imaginative psychedelic posters for Fillmore West, Avalon Ballroom and the Grateful Dead took illustration into new decorative excess. Other iconic images were created by Michael English and Nigel Waymouth (a.k.a. Hapshash and The Coloured Coat): they included posters, record sleeves and the shop front for boutique 'Granny Takes a Trip'.

Psychedelia was also embraced by Peter Max, who was famous for his posters and

KRAFTWERK

FLEETWOOD MAC

Client:
Personal work
Illustrator:
Marcus Oakley
Title:
Favourite Things

good humour

HELLO

BRIAN WILSON

decorative products. The music of the Beatles provided the soundtrack for many of the iconic graphic images of the decade, including George Dunning and Heinz Edelmann's animated film *Yellow Submarine* and Peter Blake's cover for *Sgt. Pepper's Lonely Hearts Club Band*.

In recent years illustration has become increasingly popular and favoured over photography in many contexts. This lo-fi handcrafted renaissance has taken place due to the rise in independent publishers and micro markets, together with a reaction against the Modernist style, digital graphic design and photography of the 1990s. Commercial sectors such as advertising, fashion, music, design and publishing are now looking for the personal, the warm, the humorous, the abstract and the decorative to sell and promote their products and brands.

The intertwined decoration of expressive flowing lines and patterns are very much back in vogue. The flowing calligraphic line of 17th- and 18th-century Japanese art

(Right)
A selection from the page of the Julie Verhoeven special issue illustrated Ape magazine.

A decorative vinyl Record (below) and New Orleans jazzman (left) by Jon Burgerman.

that inspired Art Nouveau, Beardsley, Mucha, Bonnard, The Beggarstaff Brothers and Steinberg's drawings has returned. There is also a postmodern fascination with retro 1960s, 1970s and 1980s graphic art and Japanese manga and animé. Ornament has always been one element in illustration, from the Illuminated manuscripts to contemporary biro abstractions and digital vector arabesques.

For some illustrators, the decorative aspect of their work is fundamental. However, in a subject area as rich and diverse as illustration, there are many points of view. Individual perspectives on form, style, visual language and content are as eclectic and contradictory as in any form of visual art.

Publishing formats for illustrators in the 21st century have also been extended into new media, websites and animation. In the fashion industry illustration is appearing everywhere from point of sale, online shops, window displays and home furnishings to fabrics, accessories and interior decoration. Exemplars in this expanding field include Jason Brooks, Julie Verhoeven, Daisy de Villeneuve, Robert Ryan, Natasha Law, Florence Manlik and Jasper Goodall.

By consulting contemporary illustrators from all over the world who operate in a broad range of contexts – the music industry, advertising, design, editorial, fashion, internet, animation, street art, reportage, satire and narrative – a kaleidoscopic picture emerges. Challenging, original, intelligent, subtle and compelling work is being created in all these genres and contexts.

THINKING VISUALLY: THE DECORATIVE

Social Comment

'One cannot create an art that speaks to men when one has nothing to say.'

André Malraux, Man's Hope, 1938

The contemporary Portuguese illustrator and award-winning animator Pedro Lino has a set of concerns that inform his practice – globalisation, alienation, technology, the idea of progress and the relationship between the individual and modern society. He argues that 'we seem to forget the idea that commercial art, such as illustration, may function as an effective questioning system'. He sees illustration as a catalyst for social change, encouraging people to rethink and question society. Lino states that 'now, more than ever, illustrators need to take chances and create truly challenging and innovative work that will stand out and evolve the way the profession is perceived'.

Biting satire, wit and radical social comment have a long tradition within illustration. During the 17th and 18th centuries, hand scrolls and block books of woodcuts were created in China and Japan. The Ukiyo-e (pictures of the passing world) school in Japan was exemplified by the woodcut work of Hokusai. In Europe, rural and peasant life, folk and fairy tales and satirical attacks on authority were featured in illustrated periodicals. They took the form of 'chapbooks' (cheap books) and 'broadsides' (illustrated sheets).The storytelling and social commentary of this popular Folk Art inspired the documentary and satirical tradition of illustration.

Key figures in the tradition include Rembrandt van Rijn (1606–1669), William Hogarth (1697–1764), Francisco de Goya (1746–1828), Thomas Rowlandson (1756–1827), James Gillray (1757–1815), Katsushika Hokusai (1760–1849), Honoré Daumier (1808–1897), Gustave Doré (1823–1883) and Paul Gavarni (1804–1866).

During the 19th century there was a huge rise in urban population, literacy, new inventions such as the steam press, cheap books, periodicals and new political views. The demand for pictorial information generated numerous periodicals including *Le Charivari*, established in Paris in 1832 and *Punch* (The London Charivari), launched in 1841, and *The Illustrated London News* founded in 1842. *The Illustrated London News*, a large-format 16-page publication containing 30 engravings per issue, was by 1863 selling 300,000 copies a week. Its format was copied by periodicals in the USA and all over Europe, including *Harper's Weekly*, *L'Illustration and Illustrirte Zeitung*.

Many professional illustrators made their reputations making numerous witty and satirical documentary drawings during this Golden Age of illustration (1840s to the 1890s). They included Gustave Doré, George Cruikshank, Grandville, Honoré

Title:
Actress Jane Fonda
arrested in 1970 for breach
of the peace
Illustrator:
Ellen Lindner

19813
CLEVELAND

Title:
A Film About Us

Illustrated & Animated
by Pedro Lino

Daumier, George du Maurier, Phiz, Luke Fildes, John Leech, Sir John Tenniel, Paul Renouard, Miklos Vadasz and Jules Pascin. Polemic and graphic agitation continued into the 20th century with Dada, Surrealism, Constructivism, Situationism and Fluxus.

Graphic illustration has also been put to use by dictatorships for propaganda purposes – the Nazis used caricatures to demonise the Jews and Social Realist iconography dominated the imagery of totalitarian regimes. In the 1960s the anti-Vietnam War movement and the counter-culture generated many examples of powerful social comment, including work by Tomi Ungerer, Seymour Chwast, Jules Feiffer, Robert Crumb and Atelier Populaire posters (Paris, 1968).

In the late 1970s the Punk movement had a profound effect on graphic design and illustration as seen in the record sleeve work of Jamie Reid for The Sex Pistols and Malcolm Garrett for The Buzzcocks, and in Russell Mills's interpretation of Brian Eno's work. Graphic agitation returned in the 1980s with Peter Kennard's collaged illustrations for CND, Barbara Kruger's posters on gender and the Guerilla Girls' satirical work on the art world. Recent examples include the subvertising work of *Adbusters*, the stencilled wall paintings of Banksy and the postage stamps of James Cauty.

Reportage

In the 19th century, reportage illustrators were known as special artists and they recorded all kinds of events, from wars to famous travel expeditions and disasters.

These eyewitness visual journalists were largely replaced by photographers, although the tradition of the visual journalist has continued; for example, the illustrating of court cases for newspaper reports is still carried out today. Magazines continued to keep the tradition of reportage alive and during the 1950s and 1960s illustrators such as Paul Hogarth, Robert Weaver and Robert Andrew Parker drew pictorial essays for publication.

In 1966 Paul Hogarth published a book of drawings combined with text by Malcolm Muggeridge called *London à la Mode*, which documented a day in the life of London. In the preface Hogarth says *'how can an artist interested in his time ignore such subject matter? The unbridled vitality of the days and nights of our capital city is the envy of the civilized world. It is a paradise for our questing pencils!'* Visual essays are again becoming popular and can be seen in the observations of author/illustrators Paul Davis, Joe Sacco and Sue Coe.

The graduate programme at New York's School of Visual Arts is titled 'Illustration as Visual Essay' and the emphasis on visual journalism and authorship can also be seen at London art schools, such as Camberwell College of Arts and in the MA in Authorial Illustration at Falmouth, Cornwall, UK. Contemporary examples of the documentary tradition of illustrated periodicals include *Peter Arkle News*. Since its first publication in 1991, Peter Arkle has published 55 issues of his own illustrated broadside featuring 'stories of everyday life as witnessed by someone called Peter Arkle'.

There is a large number of self-published limited edition illustrated periodicals being produced all over the world. In the UK, a magazine called *The Illustrated Ape* has acted as a showcase for many contemporaries, including Julie Verhoeven, Paul Davis and Jamie Reid, to name but a few. Also of interest from the UK is the large format *Le Gun*, produced by illustration students at the Royal College of Art.

Others such as Donald Parsnips, Mark Pawson, Rachel Cattle and Jenni Rope are also prolific self-publishers of illustrated material. Magazine editors have also given the opportunity to illustrators to produce work commenting on the everyday. Leading figures of this editorial tradition include Norman Rockwell, who documented the 'American dream' with 318 painted covers for the *Saturday Evening Post* in the USA, and Saul Steinberg and Art Spiegelman, who worked on the *New Yorker*.

The documentary tradition in the UK has encompassed the publishing of work by many satirists including Steve Bell, Ralph Steadman, Biff, Gerald Scarfe, David Low, Fluck and Law (Spitting Image) and Graham Rawle. Contemporary social documenters have also drawn inspiration from the expressive works of Kathe Köllwitz, Max Beckmann and George Grosz. A powerful representative of this tradition is British illustrator Sue Coe, whose dark and personal illustrations have appeared in the *New York Times* and the *New Yorker*, and in gallery exhibitions. *How to commit suicide in South Africa* from 1984 (a RAW publication one-shot) remains an excellent example of visceral social commentary. Her work is also presently being published in Fantagraphic's illustrated periodical *Blab!* The comic anthology *Blab!* is a leading example of alternative work within the field of narrative illustration.

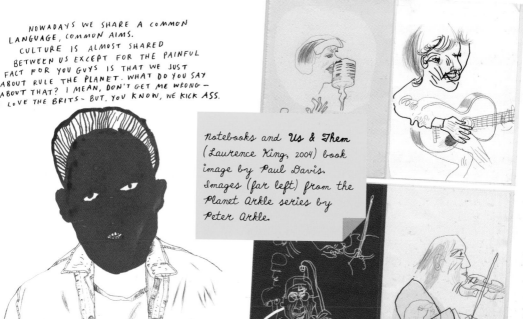

NOWADAYS WE SHARE A COMMON LANGUAGE, COMMON AIMS. CULTURE IS ALMOST SHARED BETWEEN US EXCEPT FOR THE PAINFUL FACT FOR YOU GUYS IS THAT WE JUST ABOUT RULE THE PLANET. WHAT DO YOU SAY ABOUT THAT? I MEAN, DON'T GET ME WRONG – I LOVE THE BRITS – BUT, YOU KNOW, WE KICK ASS.

Notebooks and *Us & Them* (Laurence King, 2004) book image by Paul Davis. Images (far left) from the Planet Arkle series by Peter Arkle.

THINKING VISUALLY: REPORTAGE

Underground Urban Street Art

Graffiti is derived from 'graffito', the Italian word for 'scratch', and has been seen on walls since the time of ancient Rome. The expressive application of signatures (tagging) and the spray-painting of murals on city walls and New York's subway trains became the visual manifestation of the Hip Hop subculture.

Brooklyn B-Boy and Old Skool Graffiti writer Fab 5 Freddy (Fred Braithwaite), known for his spray-painted homage to Warhol's soup cans on a New York subway train stated that *'graffiti isn't doing bad things, but we sort of threaten the whole notion of fine art, they think anything not steeped in tradition has to be Folk Art. But New York is the most advanced ghetto in the world, what we do reverberates like a satellite, bang, all over the world.'* Brand New York, ICA, 1982, A Literary Review Special

Operating outside official conventions, the underground street art movement became a rich arena for experimentation. In the 1980s pioneers such as Dondi, Lady Pink, Daze, Keith Haring, Jean Michel Basquiat, Futura 2000, Rammellzee, Robert Combas, Hervé Di Rosa, Kenny Scharf and The Urbanites (Wigan and Yuval) explored new approaches and contexts for this graphic street art. Embedded in underground urban subcultures, they painted and drew murals, self-published and exhibited their artworks in alternative venues and nightclubs, as well as in commercial art galleries.

The ephemeral transitory and improvised nature of street art can be seen in the drawings of SAMO (Jean Michel Basquiat) and Keith Haring. In 1981 Haring stated *'I've always been interested in Chinese calligraphy, Mark Tobey's work and Dubuffet's idea of Art Brut. That's why I was attracted to graffiti right away. I wanted to paint like that anyway, to make lines like that. It's some of the most beautiful drawing I've ever seen.'* Future Primeval

The movement references Outsider and Folk Art, Dada, Fluxus, Situationism, graffiti, anarchism, skateboarding, semiotics, psychology, comics, toys and music from Hip Hop, Punk Rock to Indie and continues to evolve. In a world dominated by multinational corporate brands, the strategies of advertising and viral marketing have

THINKING VISUALLY: POINTS OF VIEW

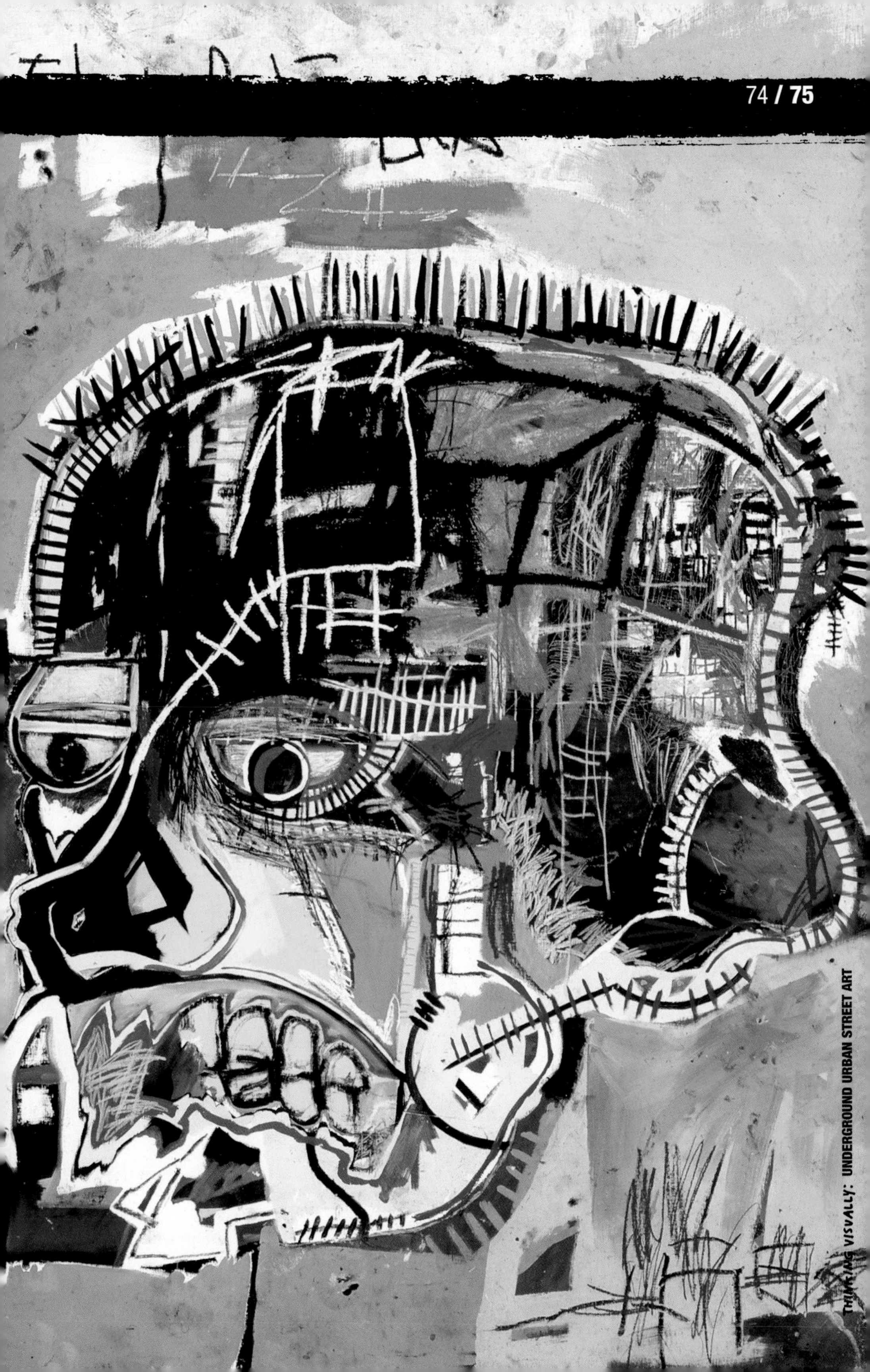

Opening of Tokyo PoP shop Jan 88°

K. Haring

Photo by Wigan of Keith Haring at the opening of the Tokyo Pop Shop, 1988
Keith Haring (1958–1990) rapidly drew hundreds of coded pictograms in marker pen
and chalk on the walls of the New York subway. His iconography depicted flying
saucers, TV sets, radiant babies, serpents, lovers and barking dogs. His many
activities included social campaigns, such as AIDS awareness and drugs prevention,
mural painting on the Berlin Wall and his Pop Shop, which sold his merchandise
including watches, fridge magnets and T-shirts.

'Untitled' by Jean Michel Basquiat, 1981 (previous page)
Jean Michel Basquiat (1960–1988) also produced a large body of work in his short
life. He began under the name SAMO, painting cryptic slogans on walls in downtown
Manhattan. Contemporary street and graphic art is an eclectic postmodern hybrid
and Basquiat has now been accepted as a major figure in 20th-century art and is
highly inspirational to young illustrators. © ADAGP, Paris and DACS, London 2006. The Eli and Edythe L.
Broad Collection, Los Angeles. Photography credit: Douglas M. Parker Studio.

been appropriated by entrepreneurial graphic artists. They promote their own brands and embed their visual signatures into the marketplace worldwide. Many critically question the effect of censorship, power and institutions in their work, challenging the ideology of the contemporary paradigm.

Skateboarder Shepard Fairey is an example of this new breed. He engages Heidegger's theory of phenomenology in his work, marketing a brand without a product. Since 1989, his image of the face of Andre the Giant, a seven-foot four-inch Russian wrestler has been illegally fly posted and stencilled all over the world. This subversive act of guerrilla marketing, often leading to his arrest, is an ambiguous experiment deliberately left open to translation by the public.

There is a long history of images appearing in unconventional locations: for example, during the Russian Revolution ROSTA propaganda-stencilled posters and caricatures appeared as window displays; murals were also painted on the sides of 'agit-trains', taking the revolutionary message across Soviet Russia, known as 'Theatres of the People'. Large-scale murals also have origins in set design for the theatre, such as Fernand Léger's 'La Création du Monde', 1923, for a Jazz Ballet and in the projected living scenery of Piscator's 1920s stage sets illustrated by George Grosz.

Department stores around the world are now featuring live painting, performances and exhibitions of graphic art and it is interesting to look back on Salvador Dali's 1939 display on Fifth Avenue, New York. His window display outraged the public, leading to the censorship of some of the work; Dali promptly overturned the display, smashed the shop window and got arrested. A newspaper headline declared 'through the window to fame'. Dali was instantly famous in New York, becoming the richest young artist in the world at the age of 35.

Entrepreneurial 'do it yourself' illustrator/marketers are attempting to engage in the global enterprise culture on their own terms. The illustrators' idiosyncratic visual forms appear on products as diverse as T-shirts, badges, stickers, mouse mats, sneakers, magnets, animated films, vinyl figures, digital prints, textiles and in traditional and virtual galleries, as well as on the urban walls.

Independent skate and club wear brands have also contributed to the movement commissioning graphic art. A few examples include Stussy, X Large, Silas, Mambo, Gimme 5, Zoo York, A Bathing Ape, Recon and Phat Farm. This new breed of illustrator also performs 'live', drawing and painting for the public sometimes via web cams to audiences and fellow illustrators around the world. Echoing the films of Picasso and Pollock at work, action painting, Tachism and graffiti 'pieces', collaborative live painting is becoming a very popular ritual. Events such as VERSUS UK, Japan, The Big Draw, International Doodlebug day and Matsuri are attracting large audiences. Live painting also involves the illustrators working on and customising one another's own designs in a democratic yet creative process.

THINKING VISUALLY: UNDERGROUND URBAN STREET ART

Celebrity graphic artists/illustrators have attained a cult status for their work around the world. Some of the most innovative include: Barry McGee, Mike Mills, Banksy, Dalek, Stephen Powers, Space Invader, Geoff McFetridge, Coop, Mark Gonzales, Kozik, Phil Frost, Neck Face, Shepard Fairey, KAWS, Doze Green, WK Interact, Tristan Eaton and collectives such as Devil Robots, Peepshow, the Scrawl Collective and Black Convoy. These postmodern practitioners are creating experiences and challenging traditional definitions of illustration art and graphic design, and rethinking approaches to the subject for the 21st century.

Client:
Swatch

Illustrator:
Wigan and Yuval

Title:
Well schizoid, 1986

Wigan Art in Japan (1988 and onwards)

Pictures include the author live painting at Panasonic Hall, Nagoya, Gifu, Shonan Beach, Parco (Tokyo) Hitachinaka City (community mural), high school mural and various nightclubs in Japan (opposite below right).

body painting at a Tokyo Rythm Kings Party

H. UENO.

aRai action painting at the FAKE EVENT IN CAVE

KIMIYOSHI FUTORI
&
KAM TANG UK Vs JAPAN

STENCH LIVE! @
UK Vs JAPAN PARCO 03

Matsuri, Autumn 2005
Japanese festival of art at 93ftEast on Brick Lane, London, with instigators Taka and Yoshi (above) and work by JAKe, Pinky, Austin and Jody (below).

V Show featuring: NEW, Andrew Rae, Spencer Wilson, JAKe, Jody Ronzo, Pinky, Al Murphy & Lucy McLaughlan in London, 2003.

D*Face
His recent street and
graphic art is an
eclectic postmodern
hybridisation.

Black Convoy

Here are some images from the collective's London show in 2005.

Storytelling

'The illustrator has unlike the painter a primary interest in telling a story.'

Norman Rockwell

Pictures have always been used to tell stories. An early precursor of sequential and narrative illustration is the 11th-century Bayeux Tapestry, which contains a linear narrative depicting the Norman invasion of England in 1066. Another example is Michelangelo's paintings on the ceiling of the Sistine Chapel. Many great works of literature have been interpreted and enhanced by pictures; there have been wonderful combinations in history including Delacroix's drawings for Goethe's *Faust*, Tenniel's interpretation of Lewis Carroll's books and George Cruikshank's illustrations for Dickens. Illustrators have shed light on and elucidated literature, and have also written and produced their own works. William Blake added hand-drawn decorative text to his self-published and illustrated books, which were influential for *livre d'artiste* (books produced as works of art) and so many of the illustrated picture books, graphic novels and comics of today.

Sequential illustration has also provided a rich outlet for satire and social comment. An early version of the comic book was the work of Randolphe Töpffer (1799–1846), a Swiss illustrator who produced satirical pamphlets and books in the 1830s.

The first graphic novels were created by Belgian political illustrator and wood engraver Frans Masereel and were described as 'novels without words'. Other seminal works include *Krazy Kat* by imaginative graphic storyteller George Herriman (1880–1944); *Zap comix* and the underground satirical work of Robert Crumb; Art Spiegelman and Françoise Mouly's *RAW*, a comic anthology first published in 1980; Terry Gilliam's animation for Monty Python and Matt Groening's 'Life is Hell' illustrations through to the works of Dan Clowes. Comics are going from strength to strength and starting to gain much more critical acclaim: for example, Spiegelman's *Maus* received a Pulitzer Prize in 1992 and more recently Chris Ware, Joe Sacco and Dan Clowes's work are also now seen as a highly respected art form.

The illustrating of children's literature covers a number of areas from pop-up, novelty, information and educational books to illustrated fiction and picture books. Often children's books are both illustrated and written by the same person. Publishers in this field allow illustrators a certain freedom to experiment. Visual narratives need to contain a fluid union of words and images paced through the story and it is also important to bear in mind the target age group and the particular function of your book, e.g. entertainment or educational. Characters in children's illustration need to be appealing and represented consistently throughout. The first picture book for children, *Orbis Sensualium Pictus* or *Visible World*, was illustrated by Comenius in Nuremburg in 1658,

we have ways of making you know how to 1.

ZEEL

MAKE and DO.

make Boar-Devil-Beast-Pig.

LETS MAKE ~
ANIMALS AND TOGGLES MADE FROM BRANCHES, ROOTS, PINE-, FIR-, AND LARCH CONES, ACORNS, CONKERS, FEATHERS, ETC. ETC, ETC.

WHEN WE WALK THROUGH A WOOD WE CAN OFTEN SPOT CONES, ROOTS AND ALL MANNER OF TWIGS WHICH FREQUENTLY resemble both human and animal shapes & faces.

NOW, lets MAKE it and DO it....

WITH EXTRA GIRAFFE

Publication:
Make and Do
Illustrator:
zeel
Description:
Activity comic

Giraffe~
SUPPLEMENT BEGINS HERE >

1 find~
YOU WILL NEED~
to search out the appropriate sticks, rushes, branches and withies to make this attractive and calming giraffe effigy~~~

and its woodcuts aimed to teach Latin and inform children about the world. During the 18th century, 'chapbooks' sold by peddlers included educational spelling and reading books, and popular tales and rhymes. Early illustrated tales include *Robinson Crusoe* (illustrated by George Cruikshank) and *Gulliver's Travels*. Colour-process printed Victorian six-penny toy and gift books later replaced chapbooks for children.

Exemplars in the genre include Edward Lear, Richard Doyle, Dr Heinrich Hoffmann and his influential chromo-lithography book *Struwwelpeter (ShockHeaded Peter)* or *Pretty Stories and Funny Pictures for Little Children*, 1846. These strange drawings and verses were intended to be an ironic parody on moral issues. Other key illustrators include Randolph Caldecott, Walter Crane, Kate Greenaway, Beatrix Potter, Arthur Rackham, William Heath Robinson, N. C. Wyeth, Edmund Dulac, Howard Pyle, Maurice Sendak, Edward Ardizzone and Quentin Blake. Children's books are often produced in a series and feature bold use of colour and intelligent design. Many historical examples have become highly collectible and the genre is going through something of a renaissance, as seen in the popularity of books illustrated by J. Otto Siebold and Sara Fanelli.

Annabelle Hartmann

Illustrator Annabelle Hartmann says that stories about kings and stories about elephants have fascinated her since childhood, so she combined the two together to produce her own children's book *As Big as a Mountain*. She says:

'Writing and illustrating children's books has always been one of my dreams.
I enjoy inventing and creating stories, small worlds of their own from my imagination to entertain myself and most importantly children.

'Inspirations come from my own childhood and of course my five nieces and nephews who, like most children, have sometimes curious likes and dislikes for stories, characters, animals, food, colours and many other things.

'By developing stories and pictures that are imaginative and colourful and entice the young reader, I feel I can positively contribute to the creative development of children and their hunger for literature.'

Marc Baines

Cartoonist and comic book publisher Marc Baines of Kingly Books was interviewed and asked to talk about his inspirations and working process in the field of narrative illustration.

'I was a voracious comics reader as a child in the mid-'60s: I'd read anything. A trip to the dentist I saw as a good opportunity to catch up with comics that I didn't usually get to see, and even at an early age there were individual cartoonists whose offbeat styles struck a chord with me. Later I discovered the names of these cartoonists. I discovered that *Grimly Feendish* and *The Swots and The Blots* were drawn by Leo Baxendale, *Thor*

Publication:
The Darkness

Illustrator:
Rachel Cattle

Description:
newsprint comic

and the *Fantastic Four* by Jack Kirby and *Spiderman* and *Doctor Strange* by Steve Ditko. Through books in the library and in a hippy bookshop in nearby Leeds I found out more about these cartoonists and discovered the worlds of early 20th-century practitioners Winsor McCay, George Herriman and Elzie Segar and later the illicit thrills of the 'underground' cartoonists Robert Crumb and Kim Deitch. These new discoveries kept my interest going as old favourite comics vanished and *Thor* and the other Marvel Comics characters fell into the hands of cartoonists with neither the visual flair nor imagination of their originators.

'By the time I went to art school I'd become bored with comics and more interested in fine art, in paintings and drawings by George Grosz, Edward Bawden, Ben Shahn and Jasper Johns. Comics in any case were discouraged, even in the illustration department. My interest was reawakened by the emergence of Art Spiegelman's *RAW* and Robert Crumb's *Weirdo*, where artists had taken up the comics medium to tell new

kinds of stories with an engaging range of styles and expression. I'd drawn my own comics with biro on typing paper when I was a kid – the *Faceless Man* (a kind of *Doctor Strange* rip-off) and *Zap-man* (a silly superhero parody) – but now I felt I had something to bring to the medium, influenced not just by my favourite childhood cartoonists and the art I'd been studying, but by Punk Rock, politics, auteur cinema, early TV situation comedies, animation, Philip K. Dick science fiction, Flannery O'Connor's tales of the Deep South, architecture, ancient and modern, walks and bus journeys and countless other things that have worked their way into my storytelling.

'Writing comics usually involves some research in the initial stages. For *The Romans in Britain* series, the initial idea came from thinking about recent immigration to the UK and issues surrounding media coverage, cultural enrichment, etc. The title was appropriated from the controversial 1980 Howard Brenton play.'

(Right)
Annabelle Hartmann's *As Big as a Mountain* is a children's book published by Pavilion Children's Books, 2003.

Title:
Cuzick's RapSoundBurger
Illustrator:
JAKe
Record company:
Handcuts, Japan

The images over the next four pages follow the working process of *The Romans in Britain* by Marc Baines.

MERCVRY, I PLEAD THY INDVLGENCE. GVIDE MY COIN TO THE REPARATIVE APERTVRE!
RED, FABIVS, SHALL REPLENISH THY PURSE!
RED, THOV SAY?
GIDDY VP, THOV NAG!
RECAPTVRE MY SQVANDERED STIPEND, RED, AND I SHALL WREATH THY TINY CHEST WITH GARLANDS!
GO, BLVE, GO! GO! GO!
YEA! BY MERCVRY'S PLVMED PVDDING BOWL, I TRIVMPH!
TO THE VICTOR THE SPOILS!
COME TO PATER FABIVS, MY SWEET COINAGE!
NOTHING!
3

'Research involved reading a 1945 Pelican Classic *Britains Under the Romans* and *Rome 753BC–AD180*, watching *Caesar and Cleopatra* with Claude Rains, looking at drawings I'd previously made from museum visits and using Google image search. From there I started piecing the script together with short scenes and working on back stories for the characters, accompanied by drawings and rough "model sheets".

'Something I wanted to use was a reparatory of characters outside of the four main characters, a few 'types' or archetypes that would reappear in different guises in successive episodes. I was thinking of the Jack Benny TV show and how they would have actors like Mel Blanc show up every week; he'd have a different name and occupation, but be playing more or less the same character.

'I'll write a rough plot then sketch it out page by page using small "thumbnail" layouts to see how the story might be told visually, using three tiers of panels of differing sizes. I'll work on dialogue and narrative captions, and how to economically ensure that text and image are not repeating the same information, but each adding a new layer of information to propel the story from panel to panel.

'I then start on the actual pages (usually 140 per cent larger than the printed image will appear), first drawing the panel borders and guides for the lettering with a ruler. Then I draw everything with an HB pencil and finally, using acrylic indian ink, sable brushes and pens finish the artwork, ready to be scanned or photographed.

'Since the collapse of the publisher Slab-O-Concrete in the late 1990s there have been no real outlets for non-genre comics in the UK and my recent work has been for comics published in the USA. As a co-partner in Vesuvius Records I'd commissioned work for several book collections of comics that we packaged with CDs and tapes, and in 2003 I decided to start a new imprint to publish a series of books by UK cartoonists like John Bagnall, Ed Pinsent and Chris Reynolds, who had been self-publishing small numbers of comics with minimal distribution since the disappearance of their major outlet, *Escape Magazine,* in the early 1990s.

'I felt there was room in the UK for a publisher that could promote home-grown talent in the same way that Fantagraphics in the USA and Drawn & Quarterly in Canada had done for independent cartoonists there, bringing names like Chris Ware and Daniel Clowes into the mainstream. So Kingly Books was launched with John Bagnall's *Don't Tread on my Rosaries.*

'After successfully promoting its first three books, Kingly has moved on to publish work by Rachel Cattle, a fine artist/illustrator new to the field of comics, and to create a new imprint, Kingly Reprieve, to republish "lost" novels in illustrated jackets and there are also plans to publish a hardback set of John Bagnall's *Disappearing Phrases* under the title of *When Pussy was a Kitten,* as well as further "graphic novels".'

Fantastic Worlds

Hybrid, mixed-up and distorted creatures are appearing in recent illustration, from Andrew Rae's *Perverted Science* to Gary Baseman's cats with phallic noses, Marcel Dzama's goblin hybrids to Klaus Haapaniemi's quirky mythological creatures.

Historical precedents can be seen in Bosch, Guiseppe Arcimboldo, Goya and in illustrated bestiaries of mythological and imaginary creatures. In the 19th century the fantastic whimsical imagination of illustrators was unleashed. In Paris, the illustrator Isidore Grandville (1803–1847) drew transformations, visions, metamorphoses and hybrid animals, called 'les doublivores', which were featured in the 294-page book, *Un Autre Monde*, a defining work of fantasy illustration.

Other influential fantasy illustrators include Sir John Tenniel and his drawings for Lewis Carroll's *Alice's Adventures in Wonderland* (1865) and *Through the Looking Glass* (1871). The satirical, humorous and bizarre are also evident in Edward Lear's *A Book of Nonsense*, published in 1846. The tradition for the absurd and unnerving continued with Albert Robida (1848–1926), who drew strange future war machines, Warwick Goble's interpretation of H. G. Wells's *War of the Worlds* and Hildibrand's drawings for Jules Verne's *Earth to the Moon*.

Anthropomorphic creatures, monsters and imaginary worlds gradually became a whole new genre: 'science fiction' illustration. Hugo Gernsback's *Wonder Stories* became the first periodical to use this term. Illustrators such as Frank R. Paul, Hubert Rogers, W. J. Roberts and S. R. Drigin defined the visual style of this genre. They worked for publications such as *Amazing Stories*, *Astounding Science Fiction Magazine*, *Tales of Wonder*, *Thrilling Wonder Stories*, *Startling Stories*, *Fantastic Adventures* and *Marvel Science Stories* (later to become Marvel Comics). Many illustrators have made their name in the science fiction book cover area; Peter Gudynas is one of the leading contemporaries working with digital technology on his cyber punk, post-human images. The work of these fantasy illustrators has also informed the cinema, including character design, set design, animation and costume, for example, H. R. Giger's work on the film *Alien* and its sequels. Cinema has also embraced the graphic novel, with films such as *Ghost World*, *Sin City*, *Spiderman*, *Batman*, *The Road to Perdition* and *The Matrix* inspired by the drawn image.

Title:
The Fall

Illustrator:
Dan Seagrave

Description:
Poster series

THE UNFRIENDLY WOMB GREW A LINING OF THORNS TO DISCOURAGE THE GROWTH OF THE YOUNGSTER

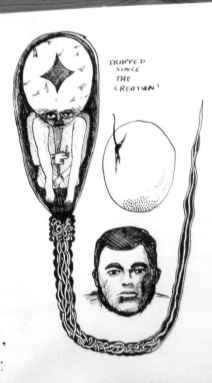

Title:
Embryo Boy

Illustrator:
Jody Barton

Description:
Ideas & research

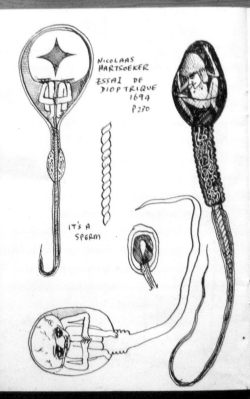

NICOLAAS HARTSOEKER
ESSAI DE DIOPTRIQUE
1694
P270

IT'S A SPERM

TRAPPED SINCE THE CREATION!

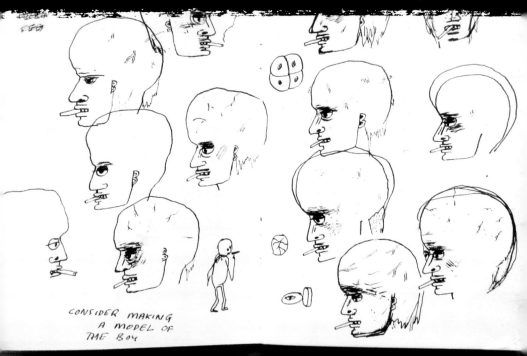

CONSIDER MAKING
A MODEL OF
THE BOY

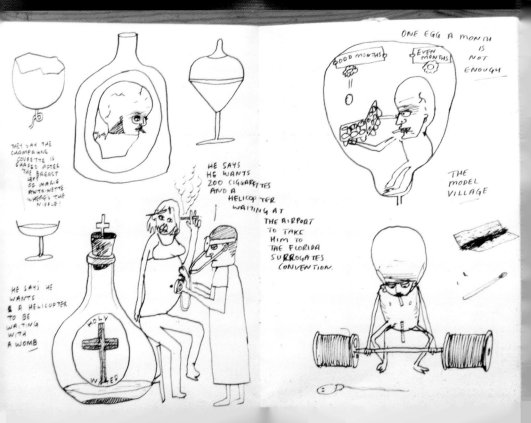

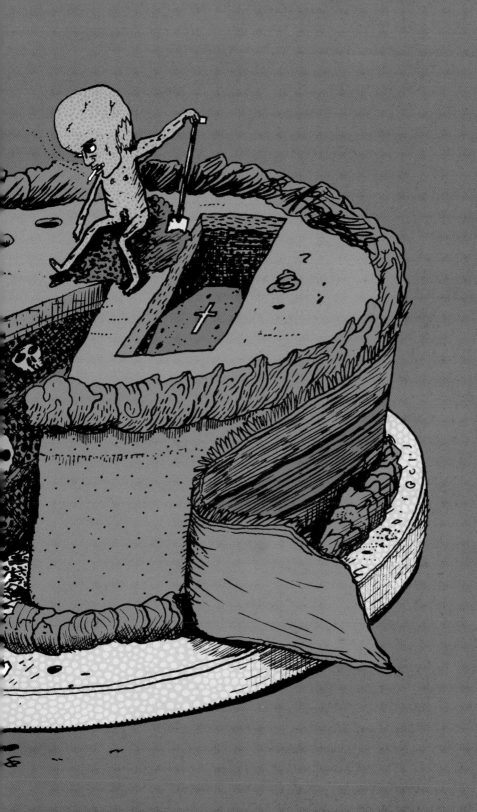

EMBRYO BOY MUST SEEK ALTERNATIVE ACCOMODDATION...

Title:
Embryo Boy

Illustrator:
Jody Barton

Description:
The printed book

HELLO
I'D LIKE TO MAKE A RESERVATION INSIDE ONE OF YOUR SURROGATE MOTHERS PLEASE...
HELLO... ?

Title: *Absolut Rasperri*

Illustrator: *Joel Lardner*

Description: *Mixed media*

Illustrators experiment with a variety of media and tools, mixing and matching to enhance their visual signatures. No medium is obsolete and anything can be used. Strong ideas, skill and craft are combined with innovative use of media. There is a huge demand for the handcrafted, drawn, sewn, cut out, hand printed and sculpted. Computers are often used to varying degrees to enhance, manipulate and send artwork and to communicate with agents, art directors and clients. The interesting combinations of media used by illustrators around the world demonstrate the variety of contemporary approaches.

Pedro Lino works with pencil, ink, crayons, acrylics and watercolours to achieve a more humane and soulful look', subsequently working with digital means. Annabelle Hartmann applies her ideas to a wide variety of products, from handmade and printed bags to T-shirts and ceramics. She works with pen and ink, woodcut, silkscreen, digital ceramic transfer prints and Photoshop. Jon Burgerman scans his drawings from sketchbooks, recomposes, works and colours them in Photoshop; he likes to use the computer as little as possible.

For the New Yorkers, Sonar On and Boudicon enamel paint on aluminium, wood and masonite, and photography, drawing and sculpture are used. Bill McConkey combines Photoshop, Illustrator, digital photography, poster, acrylic paint, alkyd oils, pencils, paper and ephemera, while for Ian Pollock it is ink, watercolour and gouache. Indian illustrator Janine Shroff also combines the handcrafted and digital using black ball pen, acrylic, a scalpel, cut outs, clay on paper and digital software. Joel Lardner combines black ink, appropriated found objects and digital software.

Florence Manlik works with pen on paper, cleaning and arranging in Photoshop if needed and Chris Drury initially works in biro, adding colours and the rest in Freehand. Joanna Nelson describes her use of media as an 'incongruous mix of hi- and low-tech. Scissors, glue, sponges, stencils, the inside of envelopes, black ink and photocopies realised in Photoshop and occasionally Illustrator to create definite shapes.'

Japanese illustrator and animator Mai Yoshida combines pen and sketchbook with Flash, Photoshop, Illustrator, Final Cut Pro, After Effects, Premiere and Dreamweaver. Paul Davis who works in most media, but not marble, adding '... mind you, there's an ideal'.

Printmaking

The following printmaking techniques have been used by illustrators with imagination and skill for many years. In illustration no medium is obsolete.

Opposite are images from a book – made completely by the traditional printmaking technique of lino-cutting – called *The Lake – A Collection of Folk Tales* from Miranda Vado. The work is illustrated by Mireille Fauchon.

'As a storyteller I have always found escapism in myth, local legend and superstition from all areas of the world. It is not simply the retelling of folk law that interests me, but the continued relevance and impact of such tales in a contemporary world bombarded by mass media.

'A self-confessed dreamer, I want to venture into worlds where explanation is found outside of logic and magic really is plausible, even if only for a select few.'
Mireille Fauchon, 2005

Intaglio: Drypoint
Drypoint is a form of engraving whereby lines are directly incised on to the plate.
A ridge called a 'burr' is left on the plate. This gives the drypoint print a soft or blurred quality. Artists who have used this technique include Rembrandt van Rijn and Jacques Villon.

Intaglio: Line Engraving
Lines are incised with a graver or burin and the burr removed for a sharp and clean line.

Intaglio: Mezzotint
Mezzotint was developed in the 17th century and is the reverse of line engraving and etching. The metal plate is roughened and indented by a tool called a 'rocker'.
The plate is then burnished to create lighter tones. The plates are printed by hand press. For examples, see the work of Turner, Lawrence and Reynolds.

Intaglio: Aquatint
Aquatint is an intaglio engraving process, which uses acid to bite metal plates.
A tonal effect is achieved instead of a linear effect. Aquatint prints tend to look like watercolour or sepia ink drawings. Often aquatint is combined with etching and other intaglio media as seen in the work of Goya.

It was often said in jest that Agnel loved his cow more than he loved his wife.

Every day without fail Agnel took his beloved animal to roam in the fields beyond the village.

As they drew closer to the lake it began to rain.

Intaglio: Etching (above)

Etching is a form of intaglio printing. Etching derives from the Dutch word 'etzen', which means 'to eat'. A drawing is produced by an etching needle on a metal plate (usually copper or zinc), which has been coated with an acid-resisting ground. The plate is put into a 'mordant' (acid bath), which etches the lines to a depth desired. Faint lines can be protected by stop-out varnish. The darkness of the print is dependent on the depth of the line.

After a series of acid bitings, the plate can be inked and wiped; the ink then remains on the depressed lines or tones. The ink is then picked up on dampened paper by the etching press. See the work of George Cruikshank and the artists Jake and Dinos Chapman.

Relief: Wood Block

Woodcuts are the oldest form of relief printing. Only the raised parts of the design carry the ink; the parts of the image not to be printed are cut away with tools such as a knife and gouge. The design is carved parallel with the grain; the strokes run with the grain (examples include the Japanese Ukiyo-e school of woodcuts and the scenes from life by artists such as Hiroshige and Hokusai).

Relief: Wood Engraving

The image is incised on to the edge grain of the wood. This form of engraving produces finer line detail than woodcuts. Wood engraving became the most popular way of printing for illustrators in the 19th century. A growing popular market for all kinds of books and periodicals required that illustrations be printed quickly and on long runs with the newly invented steam-driven presses. Professional engravers were employed to cut the drawings on to the wooden blocks.

Excellent examples include the work of English wood engraver Thomas Bewick (who pioneered the technique in the 1790s) and the Dalziel Brothers, who engraved illustrations by Dante Gabriel Rossetti and many others.

Relief: Linoleum Block (below)

This is a form of relief printing. The image is cut into the linoleum with gouges or knives and printed manually or with a press. Excellent examples can be found in the work of Edward Bawden, Picasso and Matisse.

Relief: Letterpress

Letterpress is a form of relief printing. The raised surface is made from type and is pressed against the paper. Type fonts can be mixed and a unique feature of the letterpress is the quality found when letters are not properly applied with ink. This tactile quality gives the letterforms depth, character and individuality.

Screen: Silkscreen Printing (below)

Silkscreen printing is a form of stencil printing for printing flat colour. A separate tightly stretched screen is prepared for each colour. The parts of the image not to be printed are 'stopped out'. Ink is squeezed through each screen's mesh by a rubber bladed squeegee.

Famous examples of silkscreen printing can be found in the work of Pop artists Andy Warhol, Robert Rauschenberg and Roy Lichtenstein.

Litho: Lithography

Lithography is a flat surface printing process and was invented in 1798. The image is drawn with an oily ink or litho crayon on to a flat lithographic stone.

The grease of the drawing is absorbed and then fixed on to the stone with gum Arabic. When the stone is dry, it is washed. During printing the stone is made wet; the image repels the water, but accepts the ink.

Colour lithography or chromo-lithography was developed in 1837 and involves using separate stones and drawings for each colour used. In colour lithography many tones can be produced from the same colour.

Artists who have made imaginative use of lithography include Toulouse-Lautrec, Pierre Bonnard, Käthe Kollwitz, Goya, Daumier, Matisse and Picasso.

Mono: Monotype (above)
Monotype involves the painting of an image directly on to a sheet of glass or metal. While the image is still wet, paper is laid over the image and rubbed with a roller. This pressure transfers the image. The quality of each print will vary.

Silverpoint
This is a fine delicate line drawing produced by a silver-tipped tool on paper that is coated with an abrasive. The paper holds grains of the metal, which later turn darker.

Silverpoint is exemplified in the work of Leonardo da Vinci.

The Digital Domain

For some illustrators at the leading edge of the profession, digital image-making tools are now being used as intuitively and spontaneously as traditional media. This is demonstrated in the following work of Bernard Gudynas, Catherine McIntyre and eBoy.

'The shift is from mechanical reproduction to digital reproduction and the rules of artistic enterprise and the languages of visual thinking are increasingly adopting the dynamics and forms of new technologies.' Digital Artist, Bernard Gudynas

Bernard Gudynas

The image below, 'Seven Million Hearts Beating', is an image created by Bernard Gudynas to explain a part of his visual thinking he describes as an 'art historical grid'. His compositions operate within a digital grid and an art historical grid following the thinking of Mondrian, in whose work the city is reduced to the horizontal and vertical. As electronic culture re-maps the planet Gudynas's digital grids are a metaphor for the transformations taking place.

Bernard Gudynas uses collage and photography to reflect the shifting experience of city life in an ever-changing world driven by new technology and high-speed communication, and cultural networks, business, lifestyle and travel.
'I started constructing a grid using Mondrian's painting "Trafalgar Square" (1939–43), which is sampled and mixed into the central section. Art historical references overlay the city images; Peter Blake's "Babe Rainbow" meets with William Blake's "Albion Rising" on the District and Circle line. Eduardo Paolozzi's Tottenham Court Road underground station mosaics fade into the bricks of Tate Modern. Damien Hirst's spots metamorphose into The Royal Air Force target, as used by the sixties Mods and subsequent generations of neo-Mods. Henry Beck's design for the tube map meshes with Mondrian's painting of "Trafalgar Square". All these artists have contributed to the visual fabric and look of London.'

It is evident in Gudynas's work that visual information can be infinitely developed, recycled and reproduced in a wide range of contexts, as he says, this creative re-contextualisation allows new ideas, forms and concepts to develop.

Title:
Super Bronco Battle

Illustrator:
eBoy

Description:
Digital worlds

eBoy

The previous page shows work by eBoy, who has developed an idiosyncratic digital world featuring bizarre cities populated by hundreds of characters. Its recent projects include a collaboration with the fashion designer Paul Smith and at present the designers at eBoy are working on a range of eBoy toy figures. eBoy describes its working process as 'rotation': one member of eBoy starts defining the basics, such as the grid or the resolution and another eBoy takes over and works on it. Whenever required the image can be forwarded on to the third eBoy and so on. The designers say this can last some weeks or months, depending on the amount of pixels involved. 'Rotation', they claim, prevents boredom and results in rich, layered work.

Catherine McIntyre

Illustrator Catherine McIntyre describes her working process as 'digital montage illustration' – she works from digital photographs, negative or positive film, drawings or collages and found objects. She then uses a digital camera to take macro close-up photographs of textures and uses a scanner to import images into the computer, making extensive use of Adobe Photoshop, which she describes as 'a hugely versatile, subtle and precise editing tool. Any number of elements can be pasted into a picture, in layers one on top of another; the order in which they are placed can be changed at any time. The elements can be trimmed and rotated, just as with a paper montage. However, Photoshop goes much further. The scale of the various parts can be altered, and they can be distorted, for example to create a perspective effect. Then, opacity can be varied, either across an entire layer or in parts using a layer mask. Contrast, hue and saturation are further variables. Each layer can also interact with the ones below it by using layer modes. The luminosity mode, for example, makes the layer it is applied to take on the hue of the layer below, while retaining its own tonal and contrast values.'

Catherine blends layers in Photoshop, experimenting with inversions, changing colours, opacity and modes etc. She doesn't plan the mood of her pictures, but works intuitively and spontaneously, just as in traditional collage-making, reacting to the resonances set up by the interaction of the elements.

Title:
Asha / Ice White

Illustrator:
Catherine McIntyre

Description:
Digital montage

Title:
Nestling
Illustrator:
Catherine McIntyre
Description:
Digital montage

Art Factory

The extent to which a contemporary illustrator needs to use digital tools varies. Many make use of a laptop computer, a scanner and a printer and graphic drawing tablets such as Wacom.

Commonly used software includes Adobe Photoshop, Adobe Illustrator, Macromedia Freehand, Macromedia Flash, Adobe Streamline, Adobe After Effects and Flash. Illustrators also utilise USB storage devices, digital still and video cameras.

ILLUSTRATIONS, HOWEVER, CAN BE CREATED IN ANY MEDIUM.

It is important to experiment with a broad range and choose the type of medium that is most appropriate to you. Materials used can include...

THINKING VISVALLY: TOOLS OF THE TRADE

1	SCALPELS	**23**	ERASERS
2	METAL RULERS	**24**	PAINTBRUSHES
3	SCISSORS	**25**	STAPLE GUNS
4	GLUE	**26**	PAPER
5	TAPE	**27**	CARDS
6	STENCILS	**28**	WIRE
7	TRANSFER LETTERING	**29**	WAX
8	COLOURED PENCILS	**30**	CLAY
9	PASTELS	**31**	METAL
10	AEROSOL PAINTS	**32**	PLASTICS
11	ACRYLIC	**33**	EMBROIDERY
12	GOUACHE	**34**	STRING
13	WATERCOLOUR	**35**	CERAMIC TRANSFERS
14	OIL PAINT	**36**	BADGE MAKING
15	COLOURED INKS		MACHINES
16	LINO CUTTING TOOLS		Plus:
17	ROLLERS		LETTERPRESS
18	PENS		and
19	PENCILS		traditional
20	CHARCOAL		printmaking
21	GRAPHITE		processes
22	CUTTING MATS		etc.

THINKING VISUALLY: ART FACTORY

Title: *Organised?*

Illustrator: *Nadezda Lantuha*

Description: *Student work*

Illustrators from all over the world were asked what they felt illustration students needed to learn:

Drawing!

Authorship → Interdisciplinary → appropriate?
↑internet Practice Hybrid Media → adapt
Interpretation Ideology? ↗
Non linear thinking ↑ → Research ↗ ↑ communication
analyse\ Personal Visual Strategise Professionalism ↑
Language Sequence
A New Dynamic Narrative "A Pedagogical Methods
community Play Experiment" ↗ → debate
confidence Global ↗ Nurturing - History
→ imagination

illustration as an → integrity
Intellectual Adventure → ethics
Intent → art
theory
Design Skills Question synthesize incubation
inclusive Challenge the visual thinking
A Rethink Paradigm
ambition ✓ invention Subversion text&image
Perceptual & entrepreneurship Time
Conceptual Plan curiosity Management
ethos skills critical awareness
Problem Solving Transcend Content, to Value → ideas
↓international↗ Context → Critical Making
Old + New Collaboration responsibility Practice
Technology discourse autonomy↗ Society
Meet Deadlines! → Network audience /user/client
Hard Work! → edit
story Telling

1. Mick Brownfield

'They need to know the history of illustration; they need to know what's going on in our world and who is doing it; they need to learn how to draw properly and not rely on technical aids (the computer); they should learn how to understand and interpret a brief, how to work to a deadline and how to work with a client, so that he will be happy to work with you again… it's a service industry, a buyer's market and no place for tantrums. Visual thinking and drawing… Vital! If you ain't got it you ain't going nowhere.'

2. Laura Smith

'I would like to advise students to understand that computers are just another tool and not rely on them to the exclusion of all else. I feel it is important to understand the history of art and draw inspiration from that, and the things you see in everyday life.'

3. Neil Webb

'Thinking conceptually in a disciplined way – I think it's a kind of mental training to keep things concise. Recognising exactly what the brief calls for and use that as a starting point, then explore as many conceptual avenues as possible within that remit. Ultimately, try to find the most concise visual solution for each individual brief.'

4. Ian Pollock

'Fawn, grovel, press the flesh and the basic art of plumbing.'

5. A. Richard Allen

'How to think. How to draw. How to marry the two. Ideas without

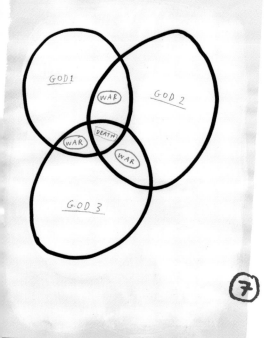

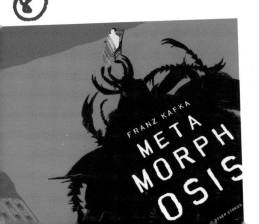

technical ability or aesthetic judgement result in sophomoric blather. Talent without original thought makes for empty virtuosity.'

6. eBoy
'Try different things, do what you like… Find out your strengths and weaknesses and use BOTH!

'A personal flaw is a very unique characteristic that can make your work really unparalleled. Look for values outside the usual illustration paths. Museums are great, but a factory is equally so.'

7. Paul Davis
'The vast majority should maybe put the hours in and discover what they can do for themselves. Enjoy the process. See things through. Try not to get too disgruntled when things seem to be against you.

'Never miss deadlines. And be aware of why the brief is the way it is – it's much easier this way. Use your spare time carefully. Don't sit waiting for the phone to ring. Do stuff.'

8. Simon Pemberton
'To work faster to a high standard, i.e., read the brief and get to the heart of it, then sort out a clear idea quickly. Unfortunately illustration is increasingly being commissioned last minute and working for newspapers especially may leave you only a few hours to do the job.'

9. Florence Manlik
'Be as personal and not influenced as possible. To keep a distance between what exists and themselves, patience, and being honest.'

THINKING VISUALLY: LEARNING THROUGH MAKING

10. Dennis Eriksson
'To invent your own style. It's very hard but pays off, and how to run your own business, to handle taxes and stuff like that. You can't neglect that.'

11. Peter Grundy
'An ability to entertain and communicate.'

12. Bill McConkey
'Get bloody educated in the subject! I can't tell you how much it infuriates me when a student knows nothing about illustration history or even the current marketplace.

'How do you expect to work in a field that you don't know inside out… If you don't know what's gone on in the past and how it is relevant to today's artist, READ! READ! READ! There is no excuse!'

13. Sarah Jones
'To keep a broad mind as to what illustration is, and not to be seduced by technology.'

14. Alex Williamson
'Obviously the basics – image-making skills, drawing/composition exploration of media, etc. The importance of developing a strong personal visual language that is allied to a strong conceptual approach – have something to say and the means with which to say it. Versatility is one thing, but they need to be aware of the "jack of all trades, master of none" approach – image-making is a craft and you need to put the time in to learn, experiment and become confident.'

DEVIL'S DANDRUFF

GUIDE TO NIGHTLIFE

By Neil Boorman & Daniel Pemberton
Illustrations by Elliot Thoburn

15. Serge Seidlitz

'You need to be devoted, live it and breathe it. Try to understand the market you are entering – it's good to know what else is going on and who is doing what, but not let it overtake your own individuality.'

16. Elliot Thoburn

'An understanding of clients' needs; to avoid dodgy contracts asking for full copyright for hardly any money; a basic understanding of the print process; that the deadlines more often than not will be tight; and not to be afraid to make mistakes and try alternative ways of working while at college.'

17. Joanna Nelson

'I try to encourage students to learn systems of organisation, discipline to meet deadlines, context to develop their own visual language unique to them, craft, to communicate about their work, to sometimes do what they are told and to get good references. But none of this means anything if you don't come across as a good person.'

18. Gina Triplett

'Students of illustration need to know how to communicate visual ideas in a manner that sets their work apart from their peers. They need to be aware of the current state of illustration, design and fine art in order to understand where their work fits within these genres. They need to know how to handle the professional end of the business that includes promotion, negotiation, communication and time management.'

THINKING VISUALLY: LEARNING THROUGH MAKING

19. Olaf Hajek

'The first thing, besides the business, is to draw and draw and create a lot of work. It's the innovative, individual work that later has to impress the client to assign the illustrator.

'Students really have to be interested in art, but in modern media, fashion and music as well.

'The illustrator has to be open minded and be able to create an individual illustration for every kind of theme.'

20. Kerrie Stritton

'I believe the biggest factor in becoming a good illustrator is to draw, whether an illustrator later works in other media, such as photography or collage etc., through drawing the fundamental skills of composition, mark-making and expression are learnt.'

21. Michelle Thompson

'How to find work, promote themselves and work to a tight deadline.'

22. Bridget Strachen

'Students need to work fast. Some deadlines are so short they leave you gasping for breath!'

23. Matt Pattinson

'The squeaky wheel gets the grease! Even the most talented/prolific illustrators have to constantly promote and update their folio to bring in the work commissions. Make lots of noise…'

24. I Like Drawing
'Do your own thing and enjoy it.'

25. Marcus Oakley
'Students of illustration need to learn to have lots of fun with what they do.'

26. Georgia Harrison
'Um, I think to keep their eyes peeled for the glorious and bonkers things that happen all around us. To keep a little bit of wonder at the world.

'Observe. Make notes. Draw. A lot.

'And I think it is important to be true to yourself. Keep it personal. Be inspired, but don't copy. Shrigley and Paul Davis have enough lame imitators as it is.

'I always think that people's sketchbooks can be richer and more interesting than finished work, because that's where the juicy personal stuff is.

'So try and retain some of that energy and charm in finished work.'

27. Paul Blow
'I think students need to continue to experiment both with technique and just as importantly, ideas. Fashions come and go, but unique and idiosyncratic ideas can transcend mere application.'

28. Anthony Burrill
'How to communicate with other people, visually and verbally.'

29. Kristian Olson

'Experiment a lot. Get into your influences and don't be ashamed of any of them. But put them away at some point so you can concentrate on your own style.

'Dive into your techniques and figure out which elements of it are strong and which are weak. Dump the weak ones. Always figure out how to speed yourself up. This will allow you to be more spontaneous and not get slowed down by your process.'

30. Rian Hughes

'To draw well. There is no substitute for a fearsome grasp of anatomy, perspective and composition.

'Only when you've learned to master the technical aspects and made it second nature – like driving a car – can you successfully express yourself.

'No writer gets anywhere without knowing how to spell, but art schools still produce graduates who can't draw the most basic things – for example, a good facial likeness – to save their sorry lives.'

31. Brian Grimwood

'I don't think it is so important to be able to draw any more… though I think it helps… a lively mind with imagination… and to remember we are all unique… people want THEIR vision… do it YOUR way would be my advice.'

32. Daniel Mackie

'My biggest shock after college was the speed at which clients require you

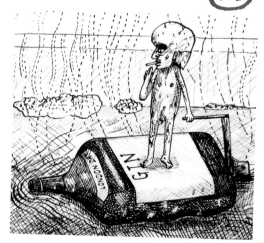

to do the work. I believe some students have six or seven weeks to do a project. In reality you get at best in most cases for editorial work one week, with newspapers, a couple of days.'

33. Jody Barton
'I think that people need to let their work take over their lives.

'The time at college is so precious. Never again will you have as much time for your ideas. Set your standards very high and always try to improve your work. Aim to do work of a professional standard at all times.

'And compare yourself not against other students, but against the best in the field. One day they may be your contemporaries.'

34. Anne Howeson
'To work with a particular (not too huge or overwhelming) idea or theme. This provides a constraint – but doesn't stop the imagination going wild. Also keep an eye on fashion, but don't be its slave. Be eccentric or old fashioned if this means being true to yourself.'

35. David Williams
'How to be curious, passionate, determined and adaptable.'

36. David Foldvari
'From what I can tell, the most important thing for an illustration student is self-confidence.

'At the risk of regurgitating an old cliché, the most important thing is to believe in yourself.'

THINKING VISUALLY: LEARNING THROUGH MAKING

Collaboration

Illustration involves collaboration with people from a range of other disciplines, such as art directors, clients, animators, art buyers, writers, film-makers, artists, manufacturers, printers, agents, distributors, gallery owners, etc.

The growth and versatility of the market has given illustrators new opportunities. Graduates from illustration courses are able to work much more as part of a team, following the lead of graphic design/illustration pioneers such as Pushpin studios in the 1960s or design groups like Tomato, Why Not Associates, Attik and Designers Republic (since the 1990s).

All over the world illustrators are forming collectives, teams that will engage with a wide range of projects from exhibitions to advertising, publicity, music and fashion. In Japan, Club King Company established by Moichi Kuwahara has acted as an umbrella for many illustrators' work with its *T-Shirts as Media* books and exhibitions, and its magazine called *The Dictionary*. In the States, curators such as Aaron Rose and Christian Strike have shown the work of many of America's leading graphic artists in their *Beautiful Losers* project (including KAWS, Shepard Fairey, Mark Gonzales, ESPO, Barry McGee and Phil Frost).

Collectives such as Peepshow, Matsuri, Wooster Collective, Royal Art Lodge, Barnstormers, Black Convoy and the Scrawl Collective are proving that there is strength (and more ideas) in numbers. Illustration agencies, such as the Central Illustration Agency, Heart and Big Active also organise group exhibitions of their illustrators' works and publish promotional books, cards and websites.

Louisa St. Pierre of the Central Illustration Agency, London, UK and currently a partner at its New York affiliate Bernstein and Andriulli says; *'By adopting a more strategic and content-driven role, illustrators have been able to create opportunities to work collaboratively. They produce work that is sophisticated, gives considered insight into copy and helps build a company's brand in a relevant, sensitive and meaningful way.'*

It is important to be aware of the rapid changes in the market for illustration. Versatility and the ability to take your unique personal visions into many media are necessary.

This requires technical accomplishment in a broad range of technologies. It also needs communication, marketing and teamwork skills.

On the versatility of illustration, Louisa St. Pierre said: *'the interactive explosion has opened up many opportunities for illustrators in animation, game, mobile and web development. Illustrators who have developed their work outside the usual parameters and are informed by a number of different disciplines have an advantage and can operate as consultants and brand strategists.'*

As examples of the new generation of illustrator/designer producer, Louisa identifies Gary Baseman and Tristan Easton of Kid Robot in the US and Jon Burgerman in the UK. From limited edition vinyl toys to editorial, TV, animation and integrated advertising campaigns, there is now a dialogue between mainstream business and collectives of illustrators and subcultural graphic art.

The Mangle (above)
Shared studio space for Rob Ryan, Dan Holiday, Hayley Newman and Danny Inwards.

Tatty Devine (right, previous page and following pages)
Tatty Devine was set up by Harriet Vine and Rosie Wolfenden. They met at Chelsea School of Art, UK where they studied Fine Art. The Brick Lane shop they opened in 2001 has developed into a multifunctional space – it is also home to the showroom, studio, offices and gallery. The following pages show their working environment and processes as they collaborate to create new pieces – from sketchbook to window.

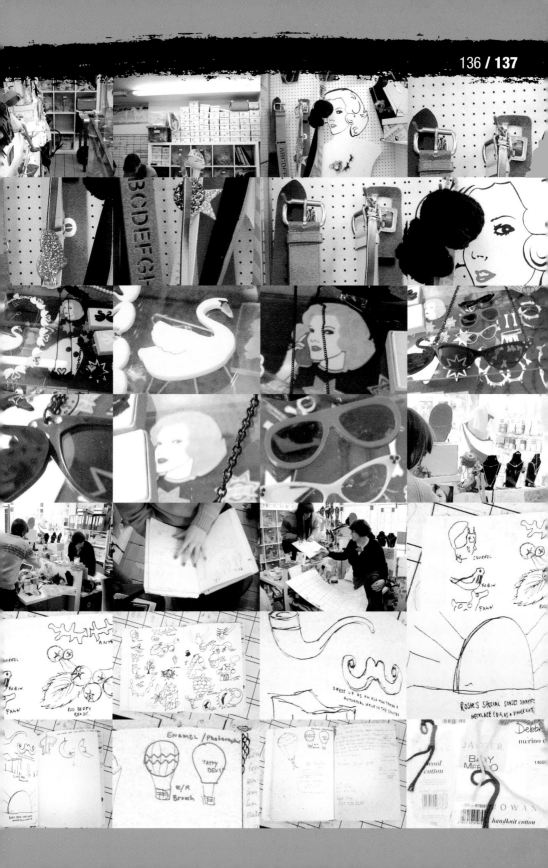

Big Active is a London-based creative design consultancy that also specialises in the management of a select group of celebrated illustrators and photographers. The agency's current line-up of artists includes: Jasper Goodall, Kate Gibb, Pete Fowler, Shiv, Kristian Russell, Genevieve Gauckler, Kam Tang, Will Sweeney, Parra, Jody Barton, Mat Maitland, Simon Henwood and Vania Zouravliov...

Big Active's Greg Burne leads the illustration department and advises on what illustration graduates need to learn about marketing themselves.

'The collaborative nature of our design work originally lead us to form lasting relationships with many like-minded visual conspirators... I remember being totally clueless myself when I graduated, so it's not a recent development. A lot of illustrators think taking an agent means they can sit at home and wait for the phone to ring which is a mistake.

'Having an agent is a partnership and as an agent I'm only interested in working with artists who are as committed to their careers as I am. Art buyers often tell me they are amazed at how few illustrators make appointments to see them. This is in stark contrast to the more aggressive approach of most photographers.

'Illustrators also need to consider the longevity of their working lives. How many illustrators have been able to sustain a career spanning 15 years and how many top illustrators earn the same as top models or footballers? Not many.

'I'd encourage all illustrators to explore the possibilities for selling their work direct to the public and to be inventive and business minded.

'Look at our industry's innovators of the last few years, creators of new toy markets, fashion labels and even virtual bands, and try to be at the forefront of something you can take ownership of in the long term.'

Title:
BFI Film Festival
Illustrator:
Parra
Description:
Poster illustration

Title:
Marmalade (2)
Illustrator:
David Foldvari
Description:
Illustration for Marmalade
magazine subsciption page

Title:
Anarchy
Illustrator:
Jasper Goodall
Client:
The Face magazine

anarchy

Title:
The Beat

Illustrator:
Will Sweeney

Description:
Cover for 'The Beat' -
a Dazed&Confused publication
- Autumn/Winter 2005

Briefs and Deadlines

Art colleges are dynamic, challenging and vibrant learning environments in which to study illustration. They build confidence and develop self-critical and contextual awareness, technical accomplishment, communication skills (oral, visual and written) and an ability to become a responsible, independent and professional illustrator. Self-motivation is essential and a wide range of learning opportunities is provided, including lectures, seminars, debates, study visits, tutorials, group critiques, workshops and demonstrations (digital, animation, 3D, printmaking, video, life drawing, photography, textiles, etc.).

Projects are set, negotiated or self-directed. Peer learning is an essential part of study and there are group, collaborative, 'live' and work placement projects.

Illustration courses have a project-based curriculum that stresses the importance of research, curiosity, imagination and personal visual interpretation. Students are introduced to the idea of working to a set brief within time constraints. Adherence to deadlines is emphasised: these range from a few hours, days or weeks and students may be engaged in a number of projects within a set unit.

The Projects

Here is a series of short project briefs designed to stimulate, develop visual thinking and engage the imagination (the deadline for each project is one week). Use of media is open (2D- or 3D-construction, found objects, mixed media); work can be either digitally produced or hand-crafted, or a combination of both.

Consider context, audience, size and impact, and composition.

You are given formats and colour restrictions to work to.

(You could make the work on a larger scale and then reduce it.)

All finished artwork is to be mounted on white board; make sure there is a border around each piece and put a tracing paper overlay to protect the work.

Label your work: name, project title and fill in a self-assessment questionnaire.

Also provide evidence of research and sketchbook development.

USE your imagination, vision, feelings, impulses, emotions, inventiveness, originality, curiosity, persistence, intelligence, energy, intuition, flexibility, commitment, drive, perception, motivation and enthusiasm.

MAKE work that can be authentic, sensitive, confident and political, considered, beautiful, oblique, convincing, bold, vibrant, strong, compelling, accomplished, contemporary, ugly, witty, bold, honest, complex, subtle, meaningful, whimsical, satirical, humorous, indirect, challenging, critical, spontaneous, radical, rigorous, resolved, refined, traditional, responsible, raw, passionate, sensuous, contemporary, coherent, complex, delicate, expressive, inexplicit, moving, adventurous, difficult, aggressive, stimulating, powerful, deep, ambiguous, and conceptual.

DO entertain, inform, educate, integrate, provoke, play, communicate, engage, excite, adorn, elucidate, decorate, evoke, demonstrate, explain, illuminate, investigate, classify, evaluate, objectify, intrigue, record, narrate, allude, convince, inspire, shock, explore, experiment, subvert, initiate, innovate, plead, hybridise, disturb, astound, amaze, simplify and synthesise.

THINKING VISUALLY: BRIEFS AND DEADLINES

Project 1 – DIAGRAM

Simplify, explain, illustrate, instruct, summarise, communicate.

Format: 6 x 6 inches. Black and white. A series of images.

Choose between the following options:

a) We Come in Peace
In 1972 an illustrated plaque was placed on the NASA Pioneer Spacecraft. This image was blasted into outer space and was intended to communicate information about the human race and Earth's position in the Milky Way to aliens. The illustration features a naked man and woman drawn in contour line, the man waving in an act of symbolic greeting. Create your own pictographic illustration; what do you want to communicate to an alien species about the human race?

b) Pictographic Narrative
Tell a story with a sequence of images using simplified pictorial signs and symbols.

c) Pictographic Map
Mobile hand-held maps are becoming increasingly popular; illustrate a pictographic map of London to introduce international students to the city. It could be a museum and gallery guide, budget café guide, clothes shops, markets, nightlife (club and live music venues) or your own personal guide to the city.

Work in line, keep it simple. Required format is the small screen of a mobile phone. Consider usability, visual hierarchy, sequence, interactivity, and simplify and communicate with your own picture language.

For these projects explore chains of ideas and symbolic languages – research ASCII (double byte characters), spider diagrams, mandalas, cartography, alchemy symbols, interface design, pictograms, schemata, ideographs, flow charts, grids, graphs, icons, family trees, notation, mantras, mazes, labyrinths, Henry Beck's *London Underground Map* from 1931, Otto Neurath's International Picture Language, Isotype, developed in 1930s Germany. Airport, Olympic Games, road signs and all forms of information design, Keith Haring, David Shrigley, hobo signs, Paul Rand, zodiacs, silhouettes, Native American languages, Chinese calligraphy, ancient Egyptian hieroglyphics (*Book of the Dead*).

Project 2 – PERSONIFICATION

Personify a product by designing a cartoon character that represents a product or an institution's essential characteristics. This can be in the form of a design for a vinyl or plush figurine.

Draw the character from front, side and back views. Examples: Pekochan, Jolly Green Giant, Ronald McDonald, football mascots, Honey Monster, Michelin Man (Bibendum), Esso Tiger, Crazy Frog, Super Mario, Mickey Mouse, Miss Piggy, Hello Kitty, Astroboy, Devil Robots, Pokémon, Blythe dolls, Smurfs, Scarygirl, Qee, LegoLand people and the work of Tim Burton, James Jarvis, Michael Lau, Takashi Murakami, Pete Fowler, Frank Kozik and Jim Woodring (KAWS).

Format: 6 x 8 inches. Full colour. Portrait. Three illustrations.

Project 3 – TYPOGRAPHIC CONVERSATIONS

Represent a series of conversations in letterforms (consider time/space/non-linearity/interpretation and misinterpretation). For example: between a stand-up comedian and the audience, a seduction, an argument, a business meeting, a debate, a monologue, a rant, a football match, in a bar, a church, at a dinner party, on a demonstration, at a bus stop, on an aeroplane, at a nightclub, in a critique, in the doctor's surgery, or gossip. Research: Concrete poetry, the Futurists, Dada, text messaging, John Cage, Saul Bass, Tomato, David Carson, blogs e.g. myspace.com.

Format: 12 x 6 inches. Black and white and one colour. Landscape.

Project 4 – MISLEAD THE EYE

Create images that play and deceive. Research: visual metaphors, *tromp l'oeil*, similes, puzzles, optical illusions, double entendres, the Surrealists, rebuses, visual syntax, symbols, puns, caricatures, Arcimboldo, 19th-century popular prints, cards, postcards, 1920s and 1930s Japanese matchboxes, 19th-century Japanese prints, Indian art, Chinese art, multiple images, hidden and reversed images, composite figures, photomontage, Dada, Punk Graphics, Dali, Magritte, Duchamp, Op Art, advertising, synecdoche, metonymy, Saul Steinberg, Jan Svankmajer, Hannah Hoche.

Format: 8 inch square. Full colour.

Project 5 – TEXT AS IMAGE / IMAGERY AS TEXT

Create an image entirely from letterforms.
Research: Concrete poetry, Fluxus, Ed Fella, Saul Bass, Paul Rand,
William Blake, Victor Hugo, Kurt Schwitters, Cy Twombly, Antonio
Tapies, Marinetti, Dada.

Format: 10 inches square. Full colour.

Project 6 – ELUCIDATE THE TEXT (ENGAGE WITH THE LITERARY)

Visually interpret a narrative: aphorisms, maxims, limericks, fairy
stories, manifestos, biographies, statistics (e.g. record breakers),
recipes, song lyrics, autobiographies, short stories, classic novels,
folk tales, myths and legends, superstitions, scientific information,
poetry, nursery rhymes, obituaries and all kinds of newspaper and
magazine articles.

Translate your narrative into a new context. Investigate an
integrated cross-platform approach.

Experiment with alternative formats and media for your illustrated
stories, e.g. Pop-up books, flip books, inserts, web comics,
animation, theatre set design, concertina, containers, graphic
novels, bellybands, French folds, advent calendars, advertising
posters, mobile phone displays, the book as art or object (e.g.
work by Sonia Delaunay, Matisse, Tom Phillips, Jean Dubuffet and
Dieter Roth).

Format: Open.

Project 7 – 'A LINE IS A DOT THAT WENT FOR A WALK'

Investigate Paul Klee's quote by visually interpreting a range of
human emotions through the use of line, e.g. scratching, beams of
light, wire, thread, charcoal. Your line could be frenzied, sinuous,
agitated, broken, soft, blurred, thick, congested, etc. depending on
the emotion you are depicting.

Format: 14 x 7 inches. Landscape. Full colour. Series.

THINKING VISUALLY: METHOD IN THE MADNESS

Project 8 – MAKE TWO IMAGES

Create two images, one representing the word 'Hyperbole' and the other representing the word 'Meiosis'.

Format: 8 inches square. Full colour.

Project 9 – CREATING A SERIES OF IMAGES

Create a series of images that describes the following human characteristics: tenderness, sadness, fear, sensitivity, compassion, humour, desire, indifference, aggression, paranoia, ambition, satisfaction, arrogance, laziness, honesty, and love.
Edit and arrange your images into a narrative and develop them further to tell a story.

Format: 8 x 11 inches. Portrait. Full colour.

Project 10 – REPORTAGE

Reportage is observational on-the-spot drawing and mark-making. Choose three from the following list to attend.
A sporting event, parade or demonstration, market, nightclub, theatre, museum, zoo, airport, train station, fairground, pub or bar, mountain, beach, harbour, desert, shopping centre, farm, national monument or river.

Be a visual journalist: make images rapidly, compile and edit, create a visual essay. Consider the time of day, the weather, atmosphere and mood, communicate your personal emotional response and point of view to your chosen location.

Your visual essay should show your location at various stages of the day, from first thing in the morning until late at night. Capture a sense of place and psychological tone.

Format: 10 x 5 inches. Landscape. Black and white.

Project 11 – WORKING WITH THEMES

Create a series of illustrations that describes one of the following themes: The United Nations Universal Charter of Human Rights, the seven deadly sins or the elements: earth, air, fire and water.

Format: 12 inches square. Full colour and/or black and white.

Project 12 – A SEQUENCE

Create a sequence of illustrations for one of the following: a horoscope, recipe, calendar, a range of gift cards, tarot cards, a children's alphabet book.

Format: 7 inches square. Full colour.

Project 13 – THE APHORISM

Illustrate one of the following aphorisms:

'No man is rich enough to buy back his past.' Oscar Wilde

'Force is not a remedy.' John Bright

'The course of a river is always disapproved of by its source.' Jean Cocteau

Format: 12 x 6 inches. Portrait. Full colour.

Project 14 – THE EMBLEMATIC

Illustrate and design your own emblem. Research: medieval and Renaissance, emblem books, tattoo art and heraldic crests.

Format: 8 inches square. Black and white.

Project 15 – CREATING CARICATURES

A visual polemic that will mock, expose or ridicule: a politician, a dictator or a celebrity. Employ satire and humour to highlight injustice or hypocrisy. Research: Hogarth, Rowlandson, Gillray, Grosz, Heartfield, Steadman, Bell, Rowson…

Format: 8 x 5 inches. Black and white. Landscape.

This project could also take the form of a puppet show e.g. shadow, glove, hand-to-rod puppets – research Asian and European puppet shows and the TV show *Spitting Image*.

Project 16 – PORTRAITURE

Create a self-portrait placing yourself in an historical context. Use an appropriate visual language for a specific time in history and geographical location.

Explore issues of identity, gender, race, class, status and gather reference material.

Format: 11 x 8 inches. Portrait. Full colour.

Project 17 – METAMORPHOSE

Create a self-portrait in which you are transformed into an animal. Choose an animal whose characteristics you feel represent your nature, e.g. timid – mouse, loyal – dog, independent – cat, slow – snail, fast – shark or possibly a mythological creature e.g. phoenix, mermaid, minotaur, or unicorn.

Research: bestiaries, location drawing at zoos, natural history museums.

Format: 3 black and white 6 x 6 inch squares and one 12 x 12 inch in full colour.

Project 18 – ILLUSTRATION WITH A SOCIAL CONSCIENCE

Ken Garland wrote the *First Things First* manifesto in 1964 and *Adbusters* magazine updated the manifesto in 2000.

'...Designers who devote their efforts primarily to advertising, marketing and brand development are supporting and implicitly endorsing a mental environment so saturated with commercial messages that it is changing the very way citizen-consumers speak, think, feel, respond and interact. To some extent we are all helping draft a reductive and immeasurably harmful code of public discourse...' Adbusters, 2000

The manifesto calls for visual communicators to put their talents to work on more worthy pursuits. Create a series of illustrations for charitable causes to be used in marketing campaigns that address environmental, social or cultural crises.

Research dichotomies and opposing ideologies, branding, Amnesty International posters, Grapus, environmentalism, sustainability, multinational corporate ideology, codes of ethics, *Adbusters*, responsibility, human rights, homelessness, poverty, war, famine, education, gender, race, globalisation, consumerism, stereotypes and social cognition, and *The Green Imperative* by Victor Papanek.

Consider audience, content, context, and articulate a point of view.

Format: 15 x 10 inches. Portrait. Full colour poster and three 6 x 6 inch black-and-white illustrations.

Student work:
(left) 'Lions'
illustration by Echao Jiang
(right) 'Diagnosed'
animation by Tina Bueno

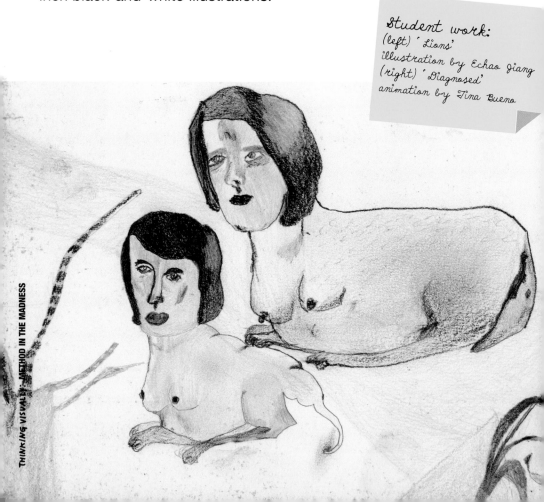

Project 19 – MAKE AN INTERPRETATION

Create illustrations to interpret four of the following words or themes: torture, save the rainforest, café life, shop sales, internet addiction, phobias, mental illness, travel, fashion.

Format: 10 x 7 inches. Portrait. Full colour.

Project 20 – MUSIC PACKAGING

Twenty greatest hits of classical/punk/mod/new wave/soul/house/ jazz/electro/ska/country/indie/rock/hip hop/garage/grime/mash- ups… Select from the above genres of music and create a CD cover to represent a compilation of 20 tracks.

Format: 5 inches square. Full colour.

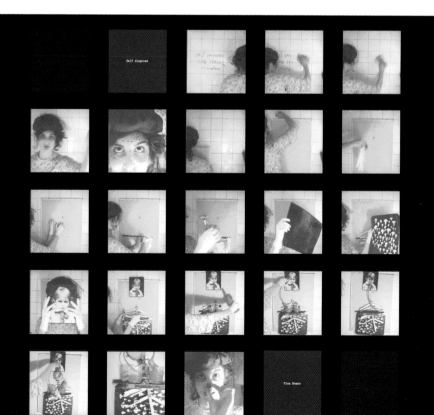

Glossary

A paradigm shift to interdisciplinarity in art and design, the convergence of evolving technologies and new global audiences, markets and concerns.

Within this postmodern critical and open-ended environment we have seen a resurgence of interest and a reappraisal of the hybrid discipline of illustration. A discipline that has always existed between the dichotomy of art and design, autonomy, collaboration and communication. Here are a few underlying principles and terms to stimulate critical discourse and practical engagement with the subject's past, present and future. This glossary invites the reader to embark on personally focused investigations from these fundamental starting points.

Abstract
In visual art, abstraction involves simplification or distortion. It does not try to be representational and often makes use of colour, form and texture. Key artists include Wassily Kandinsky, Robert Delaunay, Kasimir Malevich and Piet Mondrian.

Aesthetics
Derived from the Greek word 'aisthesis' – 'perception through the senses'. Since the 19th century it has been used to describe underlying principles and questions of visual appearance, beauty, the fine and artistic taste.

Bauhaus
'Building house'. A school of art and design founded in Weimar, Germany in 1919 and directed by Walter Gropius. Its philosophy of functional craftsmanship was inspired by the Arts and Crafts movement; its members included Wassily Kandinsky, Paul Klee and László Moholy-Nagy.

Book Art
The *livre d'artiste* (artist book) – from origins in medieval illuminated manuscripts to limited edition collections of artist prints and books as art objects themselves. Examples include book works by Eugéne Delacroix, Rembrant van Rijn and William Morris (Kelmscott Press 1891–1898) and his influence on Wiener Werkstätte in Vienna and the Bauhaus in Weimar Germany. Many well-known painters created book art including Picasso, Klee, Léger and Miró.

Calligraphic
Rhythmical and elegant flowing lines. Calligraphy means 'beautiful handwriting'. Note the influence of Japan and China on Western Art.

CMYK
An acronym for cyan, magenta, yellow and black, the four-colour process colours and subtractive primaries. K or Key is used to indicate the process colour black.

Cognition
A mental process involving the acquiring of understanding and knowledge through thought, experience and the senses.

Colour
Key developments in colour theory include Sir Isaac Newton's use of a prism, the splitting of colour and the application of the colour wheel in painting. Red, yellow and blue are primary colours. Green, violet and orange are secondary colours. The use of colour has symbolic and psychological associations which vary in different geographical and cultural contexts. Cultural differences need to be taken into account by illustrators operating globally.

Content
The subject, the technique and the essential meaning of the illustration. The illustrator and client's intention, the audience's interpretation and social cultural and historical contexts.

Context
The setting or circumstances for an event, an idea or statement. Awareness of context is fundamental to successful visual communication.

Creativity
A process that involves preparation, incubation, illumination (Eureka!) and verification (see Brainstorming).

Dada
Founded in 1916, this influential anti-art movement sought to shock and satirise society and authorities.

It spread from Switzerland to Paris, Berlin and New York. Main players included Tristan Tzara, Hans Arp, Hugo Ball, John Heartfield, George Grosz and Raoul Hausmann.

Eidetic
The vivid recalling of visual images in extraordinary detail.

Gesamtkunstwerk
'The total work of art'. A late 19th-century German word associated with the work of Richard Wagner. A synthesis of art, music, theatre, poetry and architecture. Evident in Futurism, Dada, the ballets of Sergei Diaghilev and Oskar Schlemmer's work at the Bauhaus through to contemporary performance and multimedia events.

Gestalt
The organised whole that is perceived as more than the sum of its parts. Gestalt's properties include similarity, continuation, proximity and closure.

Holistic
That the parts of something are interconnected and explicable only through the reference to the whole.

Iconography
The interpretation or study of images and symbols used in a specific cultural context.

Image
A representation or likeness, a 13th-century middle English word from the Latin 'imago'; related to imitate or copy. Image and image-making are words often used in graphic design, advertising, PR, the music industry and politics.

Imagination
The ability to form new ideas, concepts and images that do not exist at present. A creative and resourceful faculty essential to visualise and solve communication problems.

Intuitive
What you feel to be true even without conscious reasoning. Instinctive thought.

Japonisme
Japanese arts influence on Western art, e.g. late 19th-century influence of Ukiyo-e prints on the Impressionists and the work of Pierre Bonnard, Edgar Degas, Henri de Toulouse-Lautrec and Aubrey Beardsley. Japanese art continues to influence contemporary Western art (Manga, Animé, Superflat etc).

JPEG
Joint Photographic Experts Group. Compressed data standard used for sending an attachment file.

Originality
Thinking creatively and independently, creating art that is authentic, innovative, significant, unusual and new (was important to Modern art and is questioned by postmodernist contemporary art).

Perception
Awareness through the senses; seeing, hearing, being intuitive and using insight. (Visual perception, e.g. the analysis of personality using Rorschach test).

Phenomenology
The study of consciousness and the objects of direct experience. A phenomenon is a cause or explanation that is in question.

Physiognomy
Facial features or expression regarded as indicative of a person's character. The judging of character from facial characteristics (employed in caricature).

Postmodernism
A late 20th-century concept in art, architecture, graphic arts and criticism. The self-conscious pastiche of historical styles, the mixing of conventions and media, a critical distrust of theories, the questioning of originality, the convergence of disciplines. Involves ambiguity, games, play, decoration, symbolism, humour and irony. Key writers include Jean-François Lyotard, Roland Barthes, Jean Baudrillard and Dick Hebdige.

Rationale
A set of reasons for a course of action or a belief. From the Latin 'Rationalis' – endowed with reason.

Reportage
From the French word 'reporter': to carry back. The reporting of news events by the press. Before the widespread use of photography, illustrators were working as visual journalists or 'specials' documenting events. Pictorial essays continue to be published today in magazines and in the form of graphic novels. Examples include Paul Hogarth, Robert Weaver and Joe Sacco.

Research
Establishing new conclusions through systematic study.

Saccades
Rapid movements of the eye between fixation points generated by looking, thinking and drawing.

Semiotics
The study of signs and symbols such as images, sounds, media, words, body language, objects, their uses and interpretations. (See Ferdinand de Saussure and Charles Sanders Peirce.)

Serendipity
Events occurring by chance in a beneficial way. Employed in collage, montage, assemblage and automatic drawing.

Thinking
Convergent thinking: the following of well established patterns of thought. Divergent thinking: use of unfamiliar premises and the avoidance of limiting assumptions. Both thinking processes are utilised in illustration and combine the analytical and logical with the imaginative, intuitive and critical.

TIFF
Tagged Image File Format, used for high-resolution bitmapped images.

Thank you to the *New Oxford Dictionary* for the clarification of some of these terms.

THINKING VISUALLY: GLOSSARY

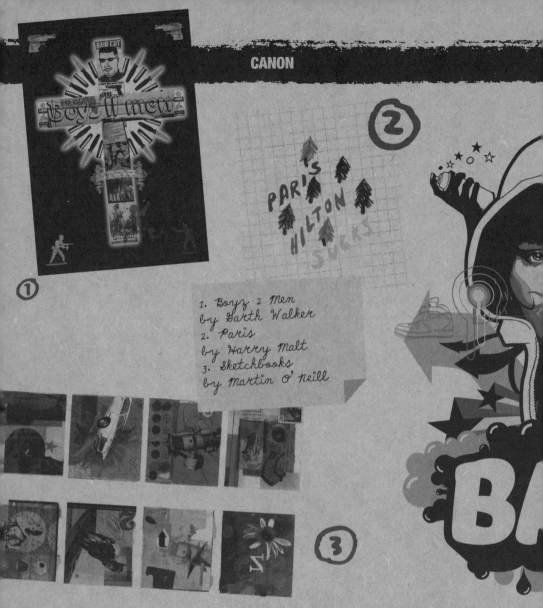

1. Boyz 2 Men
by Garth Walker
2. Paris
by Harry Malt
3. Sketchbooks
by Martin O'Neill

A canon of key artists and illustrators whose drawings have captured life with penetrating personal vision include:

Guiseppe Arcimboldo, Hieronymous Bosch, Pieter Brueghel the Elder, Jacques Callot, Rembrandt van Rijn, William Hogath, Francisco de Goya, William Blake, Thomas Bewick, Thomas Rowlandson, James Gillray, George Cruikshank, Sir John Tenniel, Edward Lear, Grandville, Katsushika Hokusai, J.M.W Turner, Gustave Doré, Eugène Delacroix, William Morris, Edgar Degas, Honoré Daumier, Aubrey Beardsley, Pierre Bonnard, Edouard Vuillard, Randolph Caldecott, Henri de Toulouse-Lautrec, Paul Colin, Eric Gill, Walter Crane, Kate Greenaway, Alphonse Mucha, Maxfield Parrish, James Flagg, A.M. Cassandre, Ludwig Hohlwein, Paul Klee, Henri Matisse, Pablo Picasso, Wyndham Lewis, Otto Dix, Hannah Hoche, Max Beckmann, John Nash, Vladimir

4. Bash
by Eelco Vandenberg

5. Untitled
by Lee Forde

6. Amore No.3
by Amore

7. Untitled (Boys)
by Cosima Hornak

Mayakovsky, Marc Chagall, Salvador Dali, Frida Kahlo, Rene Magritte, Andre Masson, Rene Gruau, Ernst Ludwig Kirchner, Oskar Kokoschka, Emil Nolde, Arthur Rackham, John Hassall, Gustav Klimt, Egon Schiele, The Beggarstaff Brothers, Kathe Köllwitz, Wilfredo Lam, George Grosz, Max Ernst, John Heartfield, Edward Heath Robinson, Diego Rivera, Stanley Spencer, Fernand Léger, Frans Masereel, Eric Fraser, Edward Bawden, Mervyn Peake, L.S. Lowry, John Minton, George Herriman, Edward Ardizzone, Norman Rockwell, Eric Ravilious, Ronald Searle, Andy Warhol, Winsor McCay, Walt Disney, Jim Flora, E.C. Segar, Frank King, Harvey Kurtzman, Paul Hogarth, Ben Shahn, Saul Steinberg, David Hockney, Patrick Caulfield, Seymour Chwast, Peter Blake, Peter Max, Tomi Ungerer, Roger Dean, Maurice Sendak, Edward Gorey, David Gentleman, Jack Kirby, Alan Aldridge, Ralph Steadman, Raymond Pettibon, Brian Grimwood, André François,

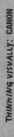

8. Sense/Memory
by Alison Casson.
9. Sketchbook work
by Jim Stoten
10. Flipit
by Gomes

⑩

⑨

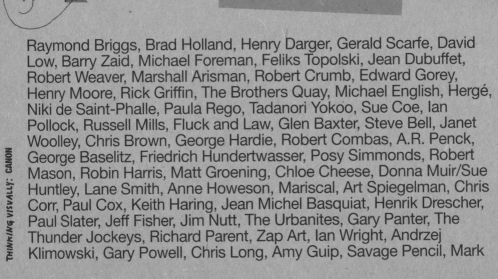

Raymond Briggs, Brad Holland, Henry Darger, Gerald Scarfe, David Low, Barry Zaid, Michael Foreman, Feliks Topolski, Jean Dubuffet, Robert Weaver, Marshall Arisman, Robert Crumb, Edward Gorey, Henry Moore, Rick Griffin, The Brothers Quay, Michael English, Hergé, Niki de Saint-Phalle, Paula Rego, Tadanori Yokoo, Sue Coe, Ian Pollock, Russell Mills, Fluck and Law, Glen Baxter, Steve Bell, Janet Woolley, Chris Brown, George Hardie, Robert Combas, A.R. Penck, George Baselitz, Friedrich Hundertwasser, Posy Simmonds, Robert Mason, Robin Harris, Matt Groening, Chloe Cheese, Donna Muir/Sue Huntley, Lane Smith, Anne Howeson, Mariscal, Art Spiegelman, Chris Corr, Paul Cox, Keith Haring, Jean Michel Basquiat, Henrik Drescher, Paul Slater, Jeff Fisher, Jim Nutt, The Urbanites, Gary Panter, The Thunder Jockeys, Richard Parent, Zap Art, Ian Wright, Andrzej Klimowski, Gary Powell, Chris Long, Amy Guip, Savage Pencil, Mark

11. Bisexual Garden
by Janine Schroff

12. Picknick
by Iris Luckhaus

13. Untitled
by Nishant Choksi

14. Nestlé Aero Ad
by Sean Rodwell

Beyer, William Kentridge, Lucian Freud, Hanoch Piven, Gary Baseman, Andrew Foster, Clifford Harper, Marcel Dzama, Aude van Ryn, Chris Ware, Dan Clowes, Joe Sacco, David Shrigley, Paul Davis, Matthew Richardson, Dave McKean, Marion Deuchars, J.Otto Seibold, Sara Fanelli, Brian Cronin, Paul Wearing, Mark Ryden, Gary Taxali, Charles Burns, Marlene Dumas, Tom Gauld, Yoshitomo Nara, Julie Verhoeven, Geoff McFetridge, Robert Ryan, Jonny Hannah, Kam Tang, Michelle Thompson, Lizzie Finn, Jockum Nordström, Jonathan Rosen, Junko Mizuno, Shonagh Rae, Klaus Haapaniemi, Takashi Murakami…

(by no means a complete canon, but a broad range of people well worth further investigation).

THINKING VISUALLY: CANON

Bibliography

Arnheim, R.
Visual Thinking
University of California Press (1989)

Backemeyer, S.
Picture This: The Artist as Illustrator
Central Saint Martins College of Art and Design in association with Herbert Press (2005)

Bell, R and Sinclair, M.
Pictures & Words
New Comic Art and Narrative Illustration
Laurence King Publishing (2005)

Berger, J.
Ways of Seeing
Penguin Books (1972)

Blake, W.
Songs of Innocence and Experience
Dover Thrift Editions (1992)

Blinderman, B.
Keith Haring Future Primeval
University Galleries
Illinois State University (1990)

Borrelli, L.
Fashion Illustration Now
Fashion Illustration Next
Thames & Hudson (2002)

Coe, S and Metz, H.
How to Commit Suicide in South Africa
RAW One Shot (1983)

Crane, W.
The Claims of Decorative Art
Lawrence & Bullen (1832)

Dalley, T.
The Complete Guide to Illustration and Design Techniques and Materials
Phaidon (1980)

Feaver, W.
Masters of Caricature from Hogarth and Gillray to Scarfe and Levine
Weidenfeld and Nicolson Ltd. (1981)

Gombrich, E. H.
The Uses of Images: Studies in the social function of art and visual communication
Phaidon (1999)

Heller, S and Arisman, M.
Inside the Business of Illustration
Allworth Press (2004)

Heller, S and Arisman, M.
The Education of an Illustrator
Allworth Press (2000)

Heller, S and Fernandes, T.
The Business of Illustration
Watson-Guptill Publications (1995)

Hill, D.
Fashionable Contrasts
100 caricatures by James Gillray
Phaidon (1966)

Hillias Miller, J.
Illustration
Reaktion Books Ltd. (1992)

Hogarth, P.
The Artist as Reporter
Gordon Fraser (1986)

Hogarth, P and Muggeridge, M.
London à la Mode
Studio Vista Ltd. (1966)

Hyland, A and Bell, R.
Hand to Eye: Contemporary Illustration
Laurence King Publishing (2003)

Hyland, A.
Pen and Mouse
Laurence King Publishing (2001)

Kingman, E. L.
The Illustrator's Notebook
The Horn Book Incorporated (1978)

Larbalestier, S.
The Art and Craft of Montage
Mitchell Beazley (1993)

Mason, R.
A Digital Dolly?
Norwich School of Art and Design (2000)

McCloud, S.
Understanding Comics
HarperCollins (1994)

Merlot, M.
The Art of Illustration
Rizzoli International Publications (1984)

Noble, I.
Picture Perfect:
Fusions of Illustration and Design
RotoVision (2003)

Rawson, P.
Drawing (second edition)
University of Pennsylvania Press (1987)

Rose, A and Strike, C.
Beautiful Losers
Contemporary Art and Street Culture
Iconoclast with DAP New York (2004)

THINKING VISUALLY: BIBLIOGRAPHY

Sabin, R.
Comics, Comix & Graphic Novels
Phaidon (1996)

Saint, G.
Head, Heart & Hips
The Seductive World of Big Active
Die Gestalten Verlag (2005)

Shahn, B.
The Shape of Content
Harvard University Press (1957)

Simblet, S.
The Drawing Book
Dorling Kindersley Ltd (2004)

Souter, N.
The Illustrator's Sourcebook
Macdonald Orbis (1990)

Thaler, P.
Pictoplasma 1 & 2
Die Gestalten Verlag (2004)

Walton, R.
The Big Book of Illustration Ideas
HarperDesign International (2004)

Zeegan, L /Crush
The Fundamentals of Illustration
AVA Publishing SA (2005)

Annuals

The Penrose Graphic Arts International Annual
(from the 1960s and 1970s)

European Illustration Yearbooks
(1970s and 1980s)

Graphis Annuals
(1950s onwards)

Illustrators Annual
By the Society of Illustrators

American Illustration
HarperCollins International

The Association of Illustrators Images Annual
Association of Illustrators

Writers' and Artists' Yearbook
A&C Black London

Children's Writers' and Artists' Yearbook
A&C Black London

The Creative Handbook
Reed Business Information

Le Book
www.lebook.com

Periodicals

Amelia's magazine
Line
Illustration
AOI Journal/Varoom
Communication Arts
The Illustrated Ape
Le Gun
Juztapoz
EYE
Adbusters
Design Week
Creative Review
Blab!
Bionic Arm
Peel
Refill
Found
Little White Lies
Lodown
Arty
Nude
Arkitip
Raw Vision
Graphic Magazine
Graphis
The Comics Journal
Art on Paper
Stripburger
Giant Robot

Websites

www.theaoi.com
www.grafikmagazine.co.uk
www.chb.com
www.societyillustrators.org
www.boutique-art.com
www.bigactive.com
www.centralillustration.com
www.3x3mag.com

Also by the Author:

Mark Wigan Total Art Global Productions
1983–1993 *Published by Mark Wigan (1993)*

Wig Out, drawings by Mark 'Wigan' Williams
Published by Mark Wigan/London Institute (2003)

Amor Infinite Volume 1
Published by Mark Wigan (2003)

Anthropology A GoGo – (A Chronicle of Cool)
1974–1984 *Published by Mark Wigan (2005)*

BIBLIOGRAPHY: VISUALLY THINKING

The Conclusion

In the 19th century, during the first golden age of illustration, thousands of images appeared in books and periodicals. These ephemeral images amused, entertained, informed, agitated and educated the public. Critics and artists argued that much of this work was poorly reproduced, derivative and prosaic.
The same criticism has often been applied to contemporary illustration and graphic design over the course of the new digital revolution. However, this debate on the value of high and low art is irrelevant when looking at some of the wonderful examples of illustration being produced in a wide range of contexts all over the world. Witty, humorous, intelligent and original illustration continues to directly affect people's lives and behaviour.

During the 1980s many people in the graphic design community and some illustrators embraced computer technology. It was felt that the Apple Macintosh, which was launched in 1984, would replace all other tools and means of production. Computers have offered illustrators greater control, speed and endless ways to manipulate and construct images. However, because of this, those that commission illustration have demanded instant artwork and deadlines have become shorter and shorter.

During the 1980s and early 1990s, some critics felt that traditional hand-crafted illustration was overused and was failing to visually represent the spirit of the time. Advertising agencies, design and publishing companies looked more towards photography and digital montages created by graphic designers. The fact that designers had been quicker to make use of digital technology, along with the rise in stock illustration and transition from traditional print to new media, led to a feeling that commercial illustration as an adjunct of graphic design was irrelevant.

However, the computer, new software and the internet have also been instrumental in the resurgence of illustration and a widening of its role. During the 1990s a saturation of digital effects, including cool, clean, modernist and so-called deconstructed typography, and flat vector graphic line drawings scanned from photographs dominated every facet of our visual culture.

As technology invades all aspects of our lives, corporations have looked for the human touch, the personal and the handmade to visually represent their products and brands. The celebration of computer trickery has diminished and there is now a reappraisal of illustration and craft. As in graphic design, a new critical discourse has taken place in illustration, with an inclusive approach that accepts the importance of the work of those operating in the margins of illustration, art and design. A new generation of computer-literate and versatile illustrators has reinvigorated the discipline, integrating old and new media, self-publishing and extending illustration beyond its traditional publishing heartland. Areas such as graphic novels, fashion, comics, the music industry, street and club art, children's books, magazines and animation have led the way in this resurgence.

The illustrator's role is still the elucidating of text (often generated by others) and the telling of stories in imaginative ways, however, there is also a long tradition of the illustrator as author (both writing and illustrating text). An integral part of illustration remains collaboration, traditionally with the design community and art directors, but also increasingly with the contemporary fine art gallery world and publishers. The illustrator remains a freelance commercial artist, choosing where and to whom to communicate to based on individual ethics and values.

The education of a professional illustrator begins in art college; it is in this environment that divisions and specialisms are introduced. Illustration is often seen as occupying an area (or corridor) between fine art and design and is usually considered as a pathway within the sphere of visual communication. The demand for illustration courses remains high; the subject's new inclusive and interdisciplinary approach proving very attractive.

Courses offer fundamental skills in image-making with traditional media and also embrace everything that new technology has to offer. Illustration students exploit every opportunity and resource across art and design areas including printmaking, computing, life drawing, photography, typography to moving image etc. With the blurring of disciplinary boundaries, students from all areas of art and design are attracted to fundamental aspects of the illustrative process, such as narrative, engaging with content and telling personal stories. It is within this postmodern complex and hybrid environment that illustrators are asserting themselves.

The huge rise in new media and inventions supported by the continuing expansion of the internet is opening up opportunities for illustrators to engage with visual content in new ways and in global markets. Illustrators are still working in collaboration with creative directors in advertising agencies, design consultancies and with the publishing industry where demand is high. They are also establishing their own companies, agencies and cooperatives, contributing to visual culture in official and unofficial contexts.

Growing numbers of illustrators are becoming authors of their own products, which they design, manufacture, market and distribute on the internet. The versatility of the contemporary illustrator can be seen in the wide range of contexts in which they are working and the types of products and artefacts they are illustrating.

Illustration appears in advertising campaigns, fashion design, editorial, the music industry, graphic novels, comics, animation, science, medical and botanical publications, natural history, theatre set and costume design, design for TV and film, the internet and interactive media, stamps, computer games, collectible figurines, theme parks, mosaics, community arts murals, storyboards, children's books, nightclub interior design, printmaking, surface pattern, educational books and animation, licensed character illustration, gift wrapping paper, stationery, cards, posters, ceramics, clothing labels, jigsaw puzzles, calendars, maps, diagrams, charts, caricatures, textiles, toy design, phone cards, tattoos, point of sale, live painting performances, company reports, corporate brochures, food packaging, billboards and many more manifestations.

Illustrators are also moving into graphic design, designing typography, art directing magazines, directing music videos, television commercials and making films. They sometimes become artists' agents, gallery curators and art buyers for publishing. Many enter education and become professional teachers and lecturers, or work in the community arts field.

With the blurring of traditional discipline boundaries, illustrators are also positioning themselves within the contemporary fine art world gaining gallery representation all over the world.

Throughout history, illustrators have been valued by the world as mavericks; in contemporary jargon they have often thought and lived outside the box. Many of our iconic images have been created by illustrators who have commented with political passion, humour and satire, educated, instructed, decorated and entertained. The enduring respect for the skill and craft of the handmade mark combined with personal vision, originality and ideas has not diminished. The global market is rapidly changing and illustration, one of the world's most popular forms of art, is constantly evolving. There has never been a better time than now to become an illustrator.

Cover image

Thinking Visually cover image by Mark Wigan from *Wig Out* 2003

Acknowledgements

A big thank you to Kerry Baldry for help with researching and compiling information.

Thanks to the NEW Studio for design, photographing and interviewing illustrators on location. Also to the colleagues and students I have worked with at: Lincolnshire and Humberside University (BA Hons, Graphic Design in Hull), Derby University (BA Hons, Graphic Design), Coventry University (BA Hons, Graphic Design), Central St. Martin's College of Art and Design (Foundation Studies) – Visual Communication pathway.

Basics Illustration: Thinking Visually acknowledges the insights, inspiration and support of students and staff teams of the BA (Hons) and MA Illustration courses at Camberwell College of Arts (University of the Arts, London).

This book is dedicated to The Land of Eagles and the dream that is Snowdonia School of Art and Design (Cymru).

Also a big thanks to Natalia Price-Cabrera and Brian Morris at AVA Publishing and the many illustrators all over the world who contributed images, advice and commentaries to the *Basics Illustration* series of books.

Name	Contact	Page number
A. Richard Allen	<info@arichardallen.com>	127
Al Murphy	<www.murphykid.com>	46–47, 84–85
Alex Williamson	<a.w.williamson@btinternet.com>	27, 128
Alison Casson	<alisoncasson@yahoo.com>	164
Amore	<amore@love.email.ne.jp>	163
Andrew Foster	<www.ba-reps.com>	35
Andrew Rae	<www.peepshow.org.uk>	14–15, 84–85
Annabelle Hartmann	<www.hartmannillustration.com>	26, 93
Anne Howeson	<www.chb.com>	32
Anthony Burrill	<www.anthonyburrill.com>	131
Bernard Gudynas	<bernard@zap-art.com>	114–115
Big Active: Parra, Dave Foldvari, Genevieve Gauckler, Jasper Goodall, Kate Gibb, Will Sweeney		
	<www.bigactive.com>	142–149
Bill McConkey	<billmcconkey@tiscali.co.uk>	24, 128
Black Convoy	<www.BlackConvoy.com>	86–87
Brian Grimwood	<www.briangrimwood.com>	133
Boudicon	<cacy82@yahoo.com>	27
Catherine McIntyre	<cmci@madasafish.com>	118–119
Chris Draper	<n/a>	53, 54
Christopher Drury	<rat_tits@yahoo.com>	21
D*Face	<www.dface.co.uk>	86–87
Dan Seagrave	<dan@danseagrave.com>	99
David Foldvari	<info@davidfoldvari.co.uk>	133, 144-145
Dennis Eriksson	<dennis@woo.se>	22, 128
eBoy	<t@eboy.com>	26, 116–117, 126
Echao Jiang	<echao.jiang@googlemail.com>	158
Eelco van den Berg	<eelco@eelcovandenberg.com>	162–163
Ellen Lindner	<www.littlewhitebird.com>	69
Elliot Thoburn	<ethoburn@btinternet.com>	24, 129
Florence Manlik	<manlik.florence@neuf.fr>	25
Garth Walker	<garth@oj.co.za>	162
Georgia Harrison	<georgia.harrison@the-farm.co.uk>	130
Gina Triplett	<ginatriplett@comcast.net>	129
Gomes	<stefan@livincompany.com>	164
Harry Malt	<harrymalt@mac.com>	162
I Like Drawing	<Hello@ilikedrawing.co.uk>	131
Ian Pollock	<IanPllck@aol.com>	25, 62–63
Iris Luckhaus	<irisluckhaus@web.de>	165
JAKe	<jakesteel@btinternet.com>	83, 84–85, 92–93
Janet Woolley	<www.arenaworks.com>	57
Janine Shroff	<scritchproductions@gmail.com>	164–165
Jim Stoten	<jimtheillustrator@hotmail.com>	164
Joanna Nelson	<mail@advocate-art.com>	128
Jody Barton	<work@jodybarton.co.uk>	83, 84–85, 100–105, 133